CHRISTIAN PRIMER

Louis Cassels

FORWARD MOVEMENT PUBLICATIONS

To my wife, Charlotte,
who incited the whole project and cheerfully
endured the inconveniences it entailed,
this book is affectionately dedicated.

CONTENTS

CHRISTIAN PRIMER

WHY THIS BOOK WAS WRITTEN

I have always felt that a reader is entitled to know, as soon as he opens a book, why it was written, to whom it is addressed, and what credentials (if any) the author has for holding forth on this subject. This information may not direct you infallibly to all of the books you *should* read, but it can prevent your wasting time on those which will only irritate you.

Two things, in particular, prompted the writing of this book. One was a survey conducted by trained researchers among members of leading Protestant denominations in all parts of America. It revealed that many people who are very active in church life—including elders, deacons, vestrymen, Sunday School teachers and heads of parish organizations—are confused and uncertain about the basic doctrines of the Christian faith.

The other thing which persuaded me to undertake this project was the experience of leading a Lenten discussion group for adults in St. John's Episcopal Church, Bethesda,

Maryland. The members of our group were remarkably intelligent people and several of them held advanced degrees in science or the humanities. They knew a great deal about almost any subject you can name, from abstract art to zoology, with the conspicuous exception of Christian doctrine.

These people had come to church hoping to find the bread of life. Before they were fed, however, they were put to work in the kitchen—or in the Sunday School, the women's organization, or the Every Member Canvass. They got involved without ever being instructed.

Many churches today have adult religion classes or discussion groups. Too often, however, these attempts at adult education misfire because they proceed on the false assumption that the students already know a good deal about the Bible and basic Christian beliefs. They tend to answer the wrong questions. It is not much help to a man who is still trying to work out his beliefs about life after death to assign him to a discussion group on the ministry of the laity. A woman who wants to know whether Jesus actually rose from the dead will not find much opportunity to raise her question in a class on parent-child relationships.

The longer a person remains active in church work—the more he becomes identified as a mover-and-shaker in his parish—the harder it is for him to ask the primer questions that are really bothering him. "I would find it painfully embarrassing at this point," a vestryman once confided to me, "to acknowledge publicly that I do not understand many articles of the Apostles' Creed."

This book is addressed to that vestryman, to the members of my Lenten discussion group, and to all others, regardless of age, who are seeking adult answers to elementary questions about the Christian faith.

I say "regardless of age" because many years of teaching a Sunday School class for high school seniors have taught me that young people are at least as apt, and I'm inclined to say more apt, than adults to respond avidly and intelligently to mature thinking about Christ, the Bible, miracles, final judgment, the problem of evil, and other subjects dealt with in the pages that follow.

And who am I to be taking on such a task? You well may ask, since I wear no "Reverend" before my name, and no initials save an humble A.B. after it. I am only a newspaperman who arrived at the household of faith after a very long detour through the wastelands of skepticism. Since 1955 I have written a religion column for United Press International which is published in a good many newspapers in this country and abroad, and which brings me a lot of letters from people who have questions about religion.

To find answers to their questions—and to my own—I have found it necessary to read hundreds of books by real scholars, and to talk with thousands of good Christians, both clergy and lay, who preceded me on the pilgrim's path.

It is their wisdom, not mine, that I seek to share with you. But there is one sense in which I am willing to claim what is said in this book as my own. I have tested it in the laboratory of my life and have found it to be dependable and true. With a profound awareness of an author's responsibility to the reader, I am willing to say of what follows: "You can bet your life on this."

1

FAITH IN GOD

"I believe in God . . ."

Those are the opening words of the Apostles' Creed. They are recited each Sunday by millions of church members. Many of them would feel more honest, however, if they were saying: "I *want to* believe in God . . ."

If you are one of the church members who can't recite the Creed* without mentally crossing your fingers, it may comfort you to know that a sincere desire to believe in God is nearly always accompanied, initially, by a strong doubt as to whether He really exists. The more deeply you sense your need for God, the more likely you are to fear that He is too good to be true.

If you don't care a great deal about God one way or the other, you can settle for an easy "faith" which is actually only a complacent credulity, and which can be maintained only by carefully insulating it from the part of your mind

---

* In case you want to read or *reread* the Creed, we have it printed with some more explanations at the end of this chapter on pages 20-21.

where serious thinking takes place. Or you can embrace a facile skepticism which dismisses God as a superstition rendered obsolete by "science." The latter viewpoint is fully as naïve as the former, and also can be maintained only by a rigorous avoidance of honest, open-minded thought.

How do you know God exists?

Perhaps, however, you find yourself dissatisfied with both of those alternatives. Your problem is just the opposite of indifference. You cannot be content with a hypothesis on something as important as this. You want to know *for sure*. And so you may be asking, as millions of us have:

Can the reality of God be proved?

To give you a straight and unequivocal answer at once, *it can*.

But you can only prove it to yourself. No one can prove it to you. There are many logical arguments which may lead you to the belief that God is a reasonable probability, but the only proof which can finally resolve your doubts is to experience His reality for yourself. You can do this if you really wish. That is what Jesus meant when he said, "Seek and ye shall find." No promise in Scripture has been more abundantly confirmed by the experience of Christians of all ages, including the present.

You may be tempted to shrug off what was said in the foregoing paragraph as "too subjective." Most of us have been heavily indoctrinated with the notion that anything which is really true must be demonstrable by objective means. This is supposed to be a "scientific" attitude, and non-scientists, at least, accept it quite uncritically. But as one of America's noted space scientists, Dr. Hugh L. Dryden, has pointed out, the objective proofs of science can lead only to a "partial and narrow view of life." There are limits beyond which reason cannot take us, particularly when we are dealing with ultimate purposes and values.

I have labored this point, not to belittle science or rational thought, for both of which I have a profound respect, but simply because I want to steer you away from a blind alley in which I wandered for a good many years. You can save yourself a lot of time and mental agony by recognizing at the outset that you cannot reason your way to a belief in God as a loving Father in Heaven.

THE BEST THAT RATIONAL THOUGHT CAN DO

The best that rational thought can do for you is to lead you to a belief in some kind of Supreme Being. Many people have the mistaken idea that even this conviction can be reached only through "faith"—and by faith, they generally mean a willingness to believe something illogical. But it really doesn't take "faith"—or credulity—to affirm the necessity for a Creator. All of science is based on the premise that every effect has a cause, and there is no stronger intuition of the human intellect than that which affirms that there had to be a First Cause.

Whether you call this creative force "the Ground of Being," as theologian Paul Tillich likes to do, or whether you prefer to use the word "God," belief in its existence is not an act of faith. It is merely a logical hypothesis, drawn from the clear evidence of a universe which you cannot conceive of as self-starting.

There are other purely rational grounds for affirming what a logician might call the "God postulate." There is in our universe an order, pattern, design—call it what you will—that is intelligible to our minds. All science—indeed, every routine act of our daily lives—is based on this fact. Even if it were somehow possible to dispense with the need for a First Cause, reason would still tell us that it is improbable to a degree which can be expressed only by fantastic mathematical odds that sheer chance should have achieved the intricate structure and coherent organization which we find in a single protein molecule, let alone the whole universe.

YOUR MORAL SENSE IS PROOF OF GOD

Many thoughtful people, including such disparate minds as C. S. Lewis and Carl Jung, have found persuasive evidence of a Supreme Being in the "moral sense" which is deeply implanted in human beings, and which has been present in every people, age, and culture known to history or anthropology. Attempts to explain away the moral sense as a rationalization of the conduct which man pursues for reasons of self-preservation collapse in the face of the fact that the imperative "ought" which men have felt in their breasts from the dawn of time quite often is directly contrary, not only to what they *want* to do, but even to their immediate self-interests.

More recently, the great Viennese psychiatrist, Dr. Viktor Frankl, founder of the new school of "logotherapy," has concluded that one of the most basic of all human needs, driving men at least as strongly as sex or hunger, is the "will for meaning." Man can endure almost any suffering, says Dr. Frankl, if he can see a purpose or meaning in it. Conversely, he will be miserable even amidst great luxury if he cannot relate his life to some larger context which makes it meaningful. It seems to me that what Dr. Frankl is saying—and I believe he would readily agree to this—is the same thing that St. Augustine said more than a thousand years ago:

"Thou hast made us for thyself, O God, and our hearts are restless until we find rest in thee."

WHY IS GOD CALLED "HE"?

Let's pause here for a moment and cope with a problem in semantics. It can be very annoying in a book like this to find that the author has suddenly shifted from impersonal to personal pronouns in his references to God. One minute he's using language acceptable to any rationalist, such as "Ground of Being," or "First Cause," and the next he's referring to a Deity who is addressed as a person with "thee" and "thy."

I'm aware that this trick can be and sometimes is used to slip in suppositions about God for which no evidence has been presented. But it would be even worse, I think, to avoid the difficulty by referring to God in neutral and impersonal terms. It is certainly true, as Karl Barth insists, that God is "wholly other" than man, and any concept of God as a sort of benign grandfather sitting on a cloud "somewhere out there" is untenable, even for a little child, in the space age. The Author of time and space obviously is not imprisoned in or conditioned by them as we are. To use an old theological term, God "transcends" all of the categories by which human minds delimit and define objects. But when all of this is said, it still comes more naturally to speak of God as "He" rather than as "It." And more than habit is involved in the preference.

We use personal pronouns to refer to God because we have found personality—the attributes of living, thinking, purposeful beings—the highest and most complex phenomenon in the created universe which is open to our rational observation. God, as the Ground of all being, is infinitely *more* than we can conceive when we try to project personhood to the ultimate degree. He certainly is not *less* than a living person. Therefore, we refer to God as "He" not because we hold any anthropomorphic concept of Him, but because it is the least inadequate pronoun we possess.

How do you know that God cares?

This is about as far as reason will take us in formulating an idea of God. And it is a country mile from the Christian concept of a loving Father. If we are honest about it, we cannot claim to find in the world around us any compelling rational proof that the Creator is benignly disposed toward his creatures. There is beauty, truth, goodness, and happiness in God's world, to be sure. But we also find ugliness, falsehood, evil, and pain. We'll go into this "problem of evil" more fully later. The point here is that an honest person, looking with open eyes at the world in which we live, may see in it no persuasive evidence that an all-powerful Being is watching with tender love over every one of his creatures.

This is where faith finally comes into the picture. Our *only* warrant for believing that God *cares* is that He has communicated this fact to us. It is the key fact about Himself which He has chosen to reveal to us, and it is the most comforting fact imaginable.

Faith is the faculty by which we apprehend the all-important message that God loves us. It is as hard to describe faith to someone who has not experienced it as it would be to describe the sense of smell to someone who was born without olfactory nerves. Faith is somewhat akin to intuitive reason, in the sense that it yields firm conclusions without necessarily tracing the logical steps which lead to them. But faith is much more than intuition. In the words of Karl Barth, "it is quite basically a most intensive, strict and certain knowledge."

"Compared with it," says Barth, "even what is supposedly the most certain knowledge on our side of the human boundary can only be esteemed a hypothesis."

FAITH CALLS FOR A DIFFERENT SORT OF EVIDENCE

A great Scottish theologian, Dr. John Baillie, says that faith is a "primary mode of apprehending reality," as basic and natural as the physical senses of sight, touch and hearing. It is therefore "self-authenticating."

"Faith does not mean believing without evidence," says Dr. Baillie. "It means believing in realities that go beyond sense and sight—for which a totally different sort of evidence is required."

Many people confuse faith in God with acceptance of certain propositions about God. There is a relationship between the two: faith in God leads inevitably toward certain beliefs about him, and the belief that He exists and answers prayers is certainly a leg up on the ladder toward real faith in Him. But it is important to remember that the dynamic thing called faith, which has been experienced within the Christian community for two thousand years, has never been merely a matter of believing that certain things are

19

true. Nor is it something which man achieved by his own struggles. From St. Paul to Karl Barth, the universal testimony of the Christian community has been that faith is a gift which God freely bestows upon those who sincerely ask for it. It is a sixth sense, as it were, which enables us to hear the Word which God speaks to His human creatures.

Once you have heard that Word clearly, you will *know* that God is, and that He is all that really matters.

THE APOSTLES' CREED

The Apostles' Creed is the oldest known summary of the Christian faith. Tradition holds that it was framed by the Apostles. This seems doubtful, but it is certainly based on apostolic teaching. The church in Rome was using it as part of its baptismal rite at least as early as 340 A.D., and it may have been in use much earlier than that. It is still being used in Roman Catholic, Eastern Orthodox, Anglican, and Protestant churches throughout the world, and even today, it has no peer as a succinct statement of the essentials of Christian doctrine.

The precise wording of the Apostles' Creed may vary slightly from one denomination to another. Here is the text found in the Anglican Book of Common Prayer:

I believe in God the Father Almighty,
Maker of heaven and earth:
And in Jesus Christ his only Son our Lord:
Who was conceived by the Holy Ghost,
Born of the Virgin Mary:
Suffered under Pontius Pilate,
Was crucified, dead, and buried:
He descended into hell;

The third day he rose again from the dead:
He ascended into heaven,
And sitteth on the right hand of God the Father Almighty:
From thence he shall come to judge the quick and the dead.
I believe in the Holy Ghost: The holy Catholic Church:
The Communion of Saints: The forgiveness of sins:
The Resurrection of the body: and the Life everlasting.
                                          Amen.

Most of the statements in the Creed are discussed in this volume. To what is said elsewhere, these observations might be added:

1. The clause "He descended into hell" is based on an ancient tradition (reflected also in the first letter of Peter) that Jesus visited the "spirits in prison" and preached the gospel to them during the interval between his crucifixion and resurrection.

2. The statement that Christ "ascended into heaven, And sitteth on the right hand of God the Father Almighty" should be read as a vivid figure of speech rather than literally. It is intended to convey that Christ now reigns, beyond space and time, as Lord of all creation, and should of course be read figuratively rather than literally.

3. When Anglicans and Protestants proclaim belief in "the holy Catholic Church" they are *not* acknowledging that the Roman Catholic Church is the only true one. The word "Catholic," as used in the Creed, simply means universal. But the ancient statement does have a startling timeliness for this ecumenical age, in that it affirms the essential unity of the Church Universal, no matter how divided it may outwardly appear to be.

2

BELIEVING IN JESUS

Nearly two thousand years ago, a child named Jesus was born into a carpenter's family in an obscure village in Palestine. He spent a normal boyhood, and attracted no particular attention until he was about thirty years old. Then he set forth to become an itinerant preacher—not an unusual thing in those days. He soon acquired a large following. But many of those who flocked to him were drawn by reports that he could heal the sick, rather than by his teachings.

After a comparatively brief career, no more than three years and perhaps less than a year, he went to the capital city of Jerusalem, where his growing popularity caused great concern to respectable religious leaders. Regarding him as a menace to community order, they arrested him, tried him on trumped-up charges, and persuaded a weak-kneed Roman governor to impose the death sentence on him. He was executed by crucifixion, an agonizing and humiliating death reserved for the lowest kind of criminals and traitors.

His followers scattered in terror, denying that they had ever known him.

By all the laws of logic, this Jesus of Nazareth should have been quickly forgotten, even in his own country.

Instead, he became the best-known person who has ever lived on earth. Twenty centuries after his ignominious death on a hill outside Jerusalem, his name is revered by men of every race and nationality in every corner of the globe. All events are dated from the time of his birth. The cross on which he died is displayed from a million churches as a symbol of victory and hope.

Who was he? How do you account for his incredible impact on human history?

How could the Word become flesh?

The Christian Church has a shocking answer to these questions. Theologians call it the doctrine of the Incarnation. The name is derived from the Latin words *"in carnis"* meaning "in the flesh."

Throughout its history, the Church has had to struggle against a tendency among pious people to oversimplify this most basic of its doctrines. Even today, there are many church members who think they are giving a highly orthodox answer when they define the Incarnation solely in terms of "The Divinity of Christ." But this is really heresy, and was so branded by the early Church.

What the Incarnation actually affirms is that the man Jesus of Nazareth, who was known to his disciples as a fully human person, sharing the limitations and temptations of ordinary men, was also in a unique sense the self-expression of God.

One of the earliest attempts to put this belief into words

is found in the first chapter of the Gospel according to St. John:

"In the beginning was the Word, and the Word was with God, and the Word was God . . . and the Word became flesh and dwelt among us, full of grace and truth."

This language may be more confusing than enlightening to modern readers. But it was full of meaning for the age in which it was written. Every educated man was then familiar with the concept of *Logos*, a term coined by Greek philosophers to connote the creative, outgoing, self-revealing activity of God. "Word" is the nearest English equivalent of the Greek *logos*, but it doesn't come close to conveying what the author of the Fourth Gospel meant when he wrote, in Greek, that the Divine Logos had appeared among men "in the flesh" of a human being.

Many other efforts have been made through the ages, and are still being made, to compress into a comprehensible verbal formula the fundamental Christian conviction that Jesus was truly man, and at the same time truly God.

Jesus has been described, for example, as "God living a human life," "the manifestation of God in human terms," and "the fullest expression of Divine personality that is possible under the conditions of human life."

THE PARADOX OF GRACE

Another approach to the mystery of the Incarnation was suggested by D. M. Baillie, another distinguished Scottish theologian who was the brother of the John Baillie quoted in the previous chapter.

D. M. Baillie pointed out that Christians from the time of St. Paul until now have been familiar with what he calls the "paradox of grace." They are conscious that they possess a genuinely free will of their own, that they are "not marionettes but responsible persons." At the same time, they are equally sure that whatever good there is in their lives comes from God acting in them. And they feel that they are never more truly free, nor more truly human, than in those moments when they are most dependent on and most open to God.

"This is the deepest paradox of our Christian experience, and it runs right through it, woven into its very texture," said Dr. Baillie. "I suggest that it . . . points the way to an understanding of the perfect union of God and man in the Incarnation."

In the New Testament, Dr. Baillie pointed out, Jesus is seen "surpassing all other men in refusing to claim anything for himself independently, and ascribing all goodness to God." Yet his disciples felt that when they were with him, they were in the presence of God. And he told them they were right in believing that.

"If the paradox of Divine grace is a reality in our poor imperfect lives at all," asked Dr. Baillie, "does not the same or a similar paradox, taken at the perfect and absolute pitch, appear as the mystery of the Incarnation?"

A MODERN PARABLE EXPLAINING THE INCARNATION

Jesus himself often used anecdotes, or "parables," to convey profound truths which are hard to grasp in the abstract. Here is a modern parable about the Incarnation which has proved helpful to many people:

Once upon a time, there was a man who looked upon Christmas as a lot of humbug.

He wasn't a Scrooge. He was a very kind and decent person, generous to his family, upright in all of his dealings with other men.

But he didn't believe all that stuff about an Incarnation which churches proclaim at Christmas. And he was too honest to pretend that he did.

"I am truly sorry to distress you," he told his wife, who was a faithful churchgoer. "But I simply cannot understand this claim that God became man. It doesn't make any sense to me."

On Christmas Eve, his wife and children went to church for the midnight service. He declined to accompany them.

"I'd feel like a hypocrite," he explained. "I'd much rather stay at home. But I'll wait up for you."

Shortly after his family drove away in the car, snow began to fall. He went to the window and watched the flurries getting heavier and heavier.

"If we must have Christmas," he reflected, "it's nice to have a white one."

He went back to his chair by the fireside and began to read his newspaper.

A few minutes later, he was startled by a thudding sound. It was quickly followed by another, then another. He thought that someone must be throwing snowballs at his living-room window.

When he went to the front door to investigate, he found a flock of birds huddled miserably in the snow. They had been caught in the storm, and in a desperate search for shelter had tried to fly through his window.

"I can't let these poor creatures lie there and freeze," he thought. "But how can I help them?"

Then he remembered the barn where the children's pony was stabled. It would provide a warm shelter.

He quickly put on his coat and galoshes and tramped through the deepening snow to the barn. He opened the doors wide and turned on a light.

But the birds didn't come in.

"Food will bring them in," he thought. So he hurried back to the house for bread crumbs, which he sprinkled on the snow to make a trail into the barn.

To his dismay, the birds ignored the bread crumbs and continued to flop around helplessly in the snow.

He tried shooing them into the barn by walking around and waving his arms. They scattered in every direction—except into the warm, lighted barn.

"They find me a strange and terrifying creature," he said to himself, "and I can't seem to think of any way to let them know they can trust me.

"If only I could be a bird myself for a few minutes, perhaps I could lead them to safety."

Just at that moment, the church bells began to ring.

He stood silently for a while, listening to the bells pealing the glad tidings of Christmas.

Then he sank to his knees in the snow.

"Now I do understand," he whispered. "Now I see why You had to do it."

UNDERSTANDING THE SACRIFICE OF CHRIST

To many people, the most baffling aspect of the Christian faith is its attitude toward the death of Jesus Christ.

One might reasonably expect Christians to recall with shame and mourning the fact that the founder of their church was executed as a common criminal.

Instead, they commemorate the anniversary of his crucifixion every year. And do they call it "Black Friday?" No, they call it "Good Friday."

Year-round, they flaunt from their altars golden replicas of the gallows on which Jesus met his agonizing and ignominious death. Their chief service of worship is built around symbols of his broken body and spilled blood. And they call this service the Eucharist—or "Thanksgiving."

It appears that Christians actually do, as they say in one of their hymns, "Glory in the cross of Christ."

Why?

The question goes to the heart of Christian faith. For it

can be answered only in terms of a belief which Christians have held with great assurance since the time of the first Apostles, but which they still find very difficult to define or explain.

St. Paul expressed the belief simply but profoundly when he told the Corinthians:

"Christ died for our sins . . . and not for ours only, but also for the sins of the whole world."

New Testament writers, including St. Paul, use perhaps a dozen different metaphors in their attempt to describe what Christ accomplished for mankind on Calvary. They speak of his death as a sacrifice, an expiation, a propitiation, an atonement for the sins of men. They depict Christ as standing in man's stead, accepting the punishment which man deserves for his willful wrongdoing. They speak of man as being saved, ransomed, redeemed, or delivered from his just fate because of Christ's intervention on his behalf.

GOD IS NOT VENGEFUL

In attempting to capture a great mystery within the dry language of dogma, theologians have sometimes made it sound as though God were some kind of vengeful ogre who had to be appeased by a sacrificial offering of innocent blood.

This is exactly the opposite of the Bible's teaching, which points to the Cross of Christ as the ultimate proof and supreme demonstration of God's forgiving love for all of his human creatures.

How can this be? The teaching makes sense only if it was God Himself who was acting in and through Christ. And this, of course, is precisely what Christians believe. As usual, St. Paul put it more succinctly than anyone else has managed to do:

"God was in Christ, reconciling the world unto himself."

God could not ignore man's sins, or treat them as unimportant. To do so would have demeaned both God and man, and would have made a mockery of the moral law. True forgiveness is never a cheap and easy thing: it is always costly to someone, either the one who forgives or the one who is forgiven.

What God said to men in the enacted parable of Calvary was: "Your sins are real and ugly, and have estranged you from me. But I love you in spite of your hard hearts and selfish ways. I will pay the price of your folly. I will do the suffering which must be done if there is to be a genuine reconciliation."

This is the "good news of salvation" (or, to use the Greek term, *gospel*) which the Christian Church proclaims. It is addressed to all men in all ages. Although Christ died at a specific time and place, the Church has always understood that this momentous event transcended history so that it is, in a real sense, always contemporaneous. The good news is not that God paid the price of reconciliation for certain people who lived in Palestine twenty centuries ago, but rather that He is paying it today, for you and me.

CAN YOU BELIEVE IN THE RESURRECTION?

All very comforting, you may be thinking, but how do I know it's true?

It's a good question, and God knew that men would ask it. So He answered it in a way that the first Apostles found overwhelmingly convincing.

31

His answer was the Resurrection.

There are many people who reject the Resurrection on the *a priori* assumption that it simply couldn't have happened.

It is obviously impossible to prove to anyone determined not to believe it that a particular event actually happened nearly two thousand years ago. If you are irrevocably committed to the proposition that it would have been "impossible" for Christ to triumph over death, you may as well quit fiddling around the fringes of Christianity, because, as St. Paul bluntly said, the whole thing stands or falls on the fact of the Resurrection. Either it happened, or it didn't, and if it didn't Christianity is a gigantic fraud, and the sooner we are quit of it, the better.

If, however, you have enough of an open mind to acknowledge that "with God, all things are possible"—to accept, in other words, the hypothetical possibility that God could suspend his own laws of mortality if He had a unique point He was trying to demonstrate to mankind—then you may come to understand why the Resurrection is sometimes called "the best attested fact of history."

THE STORY DID NOT END AT THE CROSS

The existence of the Christian Church is the most convincing evidence that something very extraordinary took place in and near the city of Jerusalem in the spring of the year 30 A.D.

The disciples of Jesus had followed him during his itinerant ministry because they believed he was sent by God. Then they had seen him arrested, tried, and put to death in a most disgraceful fashion. God had not intervened to rescue him or strike down his persecutors; and after all the wondrous acts he had performed for others, he seemed to have no power to save himself. The disciples had fled from the scene of the crucifixion in panic and despair, their hopes crushed, their own lives in peril.

If the story had ended there, the world would never have heard of Jesus of Nazareth. He would have been just another religious fanatic executed in a remote corner of the Roman Empire.

But the story didn't end there. Within three days, Jesus had returned to them. They were as startled to see him alive as you would be if you met on the street today a friend whose funeral you attended a few days ago. No person hearing the story of the Resurrection today can possibly be any more skeptical of it than were the Apostles when they first heard about it. The record shows that Jesus had to go to great lengths to overcome their incredulity. Once he ate an impromptu meal of cold fish and honeycomb—the only food at hand—to demonstrate to one die-hard doubter that he wasn't a ghost.

THE DISCIPLES AND MARTYRS HAD NO DOUBT

Once the disciples got over their surprise, they were totally convinced. There is in all history no example of a group of human beings who were more absolutely, unflinchingly certain of a fact than the early Church was of the reality of the Resurrection. Any suggestion that their conviction was feigned quickly founders on the crosses of the Christian martyrs which soon sprang up from Jerusalem to Rome. Men do not die joyously to perpetuate a hoax.

It is also clear from the Christian community's earliest records, which we call the New Testament, that the Resurrection did not impress the disciples merely as an awesome miracle. These devout Jews had never doubted that God could resuscitate a dead man if He chose to do so. The good news was that God *did* choose to do so, in the case of Jesus. Thus the Resurrection was above all else a divine sign and seal on the work of Jesus. It was the ultimate confirmation that he had indeed been sent by God, and that he had told men the truth.

Christian theology did not begin with belief that Jesus was the son of God and work forward to the Resurrection as a logical sequel. It began with the startling, unexpected fact of the Resurrection, and worked back to figure out what manner of person this was that had walked among men.

It is tragic that people who would come to Christ today are first confronted with a creed, or set of dogmatic propositions about who he was, and what he did for man. With the disciples, it was the other way around. All of their doctrines about Christ, as Professor John Knox of Union Theological Seminary has pointed out, were merely "an effort to represent the meaning of a salvation which had actually been bestowed and received in the fellowship men had with Jesus."

TRYING TO UNDERSTAND THE HOLY SPIRIT

"For men in very truth found God in Him," says Professor Knox. "When He said 'thy sins are forgiven thee,' the sinner knew he was in fact forgiven, and that the hold of his enemy was broken. And men and women whose lives had been empty and meaningless became, in His presence, suddenly aware of the beauty of God, and what had been a form of death became life everlasting."

It is still possible to know Christ as a living reality and to experience at first-hand his incredible power to heal, to reconcile, to make whole, and to renew.

If the Christian Church had to exist on the memories of the first Apostles, it would have died out within one or two centuries at the most. It has endured for twenty centuries, and spread into every corner of the globe, because the risen Christ has kept the promise he made to the disciples:

"I will not leave you comfortless . . . I will be with you always, even unto the end of time."

He is present among men today as a spirit free of the limits of time and space rather than as a human person who can only be in one place at a time. It is traditional to refer to his presence as the Holy Spirit, but if that ancient theological phrase causes you difficulty, it is perfectly permissible to think instead of the Spirit of Christ, dwelling within the minds and hearts of men, unseen but strongly felt and unmistakably real to all who are willing to give him room in their lives.

You can still meet Christ's disciples

The Bible teaches—and Christian experience abundantly confirms—that the works of the Holy Spirit are unpredictable and by no means confined to the institutional Church. Even the most narrow-minded Christian must admit, on occasion, that the Holy Spirit seems to be working in and through people who do not consciously profess faith in Christ. This should not surprise anyone who has read the New Testament. Jesus was always consorting with sinners, to the horror of pious types who thought he should have been exclusively concerned with them.

Even though it is possible to encounter Christ in any

35

human activity, and to love him incognito long before you know his name, the surest places to meet him are those which he designated as his special points of rendezvous with mankind.

One of them is the fellowship of the Christian Church. You may look at any particular parish church from the outside and see nothing but hypocrites and sinners. But if you begin to share the life of the Christian community, in earnest, you will discover that every parish has at least a few truly dedicated disciples of Christ, men and women who know him personally and not by hearsay, who walk with him daily, and who will be glad to introduce you to him. They are not likely to run you down with offers of guidance. In fact, it may take you quite a while to recognize them, because they do not parade their piety or boast of their acquaintance with Christ. But they are there, and if you look for them, you'll find them. And when you do you'll see what Jesus meant when he said: "Where two or three are gathered in my name, I will be there among them."

READING YOUR BIBLE

A pastor once startled his congregation by asking:

"How many of you would like to receive a personal message from God to guide you in dealing with your problems and to help you make sense out of life?"

After some hesitation, nearly every hand was raised.

"Very well," said the pastor. "I'll tell you where you can find such a message."

He reached into the pulpit and held up a Bible.

"You may have to read this book fairly extensively before you encounter the message that is addressed especially to you," he said.

"But I can guarantee that if you read it faithfully, God will speak to you through it, just as genuinely and personally as if He had sent you a telegram."

That pastor was neither a fanatic nor a fundamentalist. He was trying to communicate a basic fact of Christian experience, on which there is a striking degree of agreement among liberals and conservatives, Protestants and Catholics, ancient Church fathers and modern theologians.

"The Bible not only tells us how God sought His people in the past; it is also a means by which he seeks us out today," says Professor Robert McAfee Brown of Stanford University. "Not only are God's demands and promises brought home to us but God himself speaks to us as we take the Bible seriously. It is for this reason that we speak of the Bible as 'The Word of God.'"

WHO WROTE THE BIBLE?

Although Christians are united in the conviction that the Bible communicates God's Word to man, they are deeply divided in their understanding of how the Bible is to be read and interpreted.

Some of them believe that God (in the person of the indwelling Holy Spirit) inspired the very words of Scripture. They think of God as being the Author of the Bible in a rather literal sense, with the human writers serving as His instruments in much the same way as a modern stenographer takes dictation. The logical corollary of this doctrine of "plenary verbal inspiration" is that the Bible must be "inerrant"—that is, totally free from any kind of error or contradiction, equally authoritative in all of its parts.

This view of the Bible is the cornerstone of the theological position which used to be called fundamentalism and which is now increasingly known to its adherents as "evangelical Protestantism." It is the dominant teaching in two of the largest Protestant bodies—the Southern Baptist Convention and the Lutheran Church-Missouri Synod—and in scores of smaller evangelical bodies. It also has some followers in other denominations.

Christians who reject fundamentalism—and they constitute a substantial majority in most of the major denominations—take a different view of inspiration. They believe that the human authors of the Bible were indeed guided by the Holy Spirit, particularly in dealing with the spiritual insights, concepts, and revelational events which comprise its essential message.

But they believe that God worked in the writing of the Bible in the same way that He always works: namely, through normal human beings who retained all of their limitations and fallibilities. Thus it is to be expected that the Bible will contain errors and contradictions, that it will reflect the primitive views of the universe which prevailed during the ages in which it was written, and that it will be often at odds with the more accurate knowledge of natural processes which has been gained by modern science.

Also, it is to be expected that the Bible will show an evolutionary progress in man's ideas about God, from the harsh notions of a vengeful Deity in the early books of Hebrew history, through the sublime ethical teachings of the later prophets, to the supreme revelation of God's love in the New Testament record of Jesus Christ.

Finally, this view of inspiration can acknowledge without embarrassment the obvious fact that there are many different kinds of literature in the Bible. There is history, and there is legend. There are biographies of real people, and there are fictional stories designed to drive home a moral lesson. There is prose and there is poetry. Trying to apply a single criterion of interpretation to all parts of the Bible is like trying to play a Beethoven symphony with one note.

THE NATURE OF BIBLICAL ANALYSIS

To the fundamentalist who believes in an inerrant Bible, it seems blasphemous to subject the scriptures to critical analysis. But to those who take the Bible seriously without taking it literally, it is both right and necessary to apply the tools of literary and historical criticism to the task of extracting its real message.

During the past century, the Bible has undergone the most exhaustive and radical scrutiny ever focused on any document. Biblical critics have examined literally every word and phrase, trying to differentiate between historical fact and illustrative myth, original sayings and explanatory interpolations. Nothing has been taken for granted.

Some anxious Christians feared that this critical shakedown would discredit the Bible. But the result has been just the opposite. In the words of Professor William F. Albright of Johns Hopkins University, the net effect of modern research, including recent archaeological discoveries and extensive study of such documentary finds as the Dead Sea Scrolls, has been to vindicate the "substantial historicity" of the Bible "to an extent I should have thought impossible forty years ago."

MODERN RESEARCH HAS PROVED ITS ACCURACY

"There has been a general return to appreciation of the Bible's accuracy, both in general sweep and in factual detail," says Professor Albright. "To all who believe in the eternal value of the Old and New Testaments, it is clear that God has been preparing the way for a revival of basic Christianity through enlightened faith in His Word."

"Enlightened faith" in the Bible as a dependable record

of God's self-revelation in history has become a dominant theme of contemporary theology, both in the major Protestant denominations and in the Roman Catholic Church. The Bible is being read and studied, not merely as a record of ancient religious history nor as a source book of doctrine, but as a living document through which the Word of God speaks directly to modern man, giving him a clue to the riddle of his existence and light unto his pathway, here and now.

Why God should choose to communicate with men through the pages of this particular book is a question that Christians cannot answer. They can only affirm that it happens, and invite skeptics to try for themselves whether it be so.

Some people unfortunately try to reduce the great mystery to an absurd kind of magic. They open the Bible at random, stab their fingers at a verse, and expect therein to find God's instant answer to whatever is troubling them at that moment. The notion that Divine guidance is dispensed in such a mechanical, penny-in-the-slot manner is an insult to God and puts the Bible on a par with a ouija board.

Less blasphemous, but equally ineffective, is casual Scripture-nibbling in which the reader jumps around from one part of the Bible to another, without plan or purpose, reading perhaps a psalm tonight, a chapter from one of the gospels tomorrow night, and one of St. Paul's letters next week—or next month.

READ THE GREAT BOOK OBJECTIVELY

If you genuinely want to hear the voice of God speaking to you through the Bible, you must be prepared not merely to read it, but to study it, seriously and systematically.

"We are frequently advised to read the Bible with our own personal needs in mind, and to look for answers to our private questions," says Dr. Frederick C. Grant, a leading Biblical scholar of the Episcopal Church.

"This is good as far as it goes . . . But better still is the advice to study the Bible objectively, and write down what it teaches, summarizing the thought in our own language but without regard—first of all—to our own subjective needs.

"Let the great passages fix themselves in our memory. Let them stay there permanently like bright beacons, launching their powerful shafts of light upon life's problems—our own and everyone's—as they illumine now one, now another dark area of human life . . .

"Following such a method, we discover that the Bible does 'speak to our condition' and meet our needs, not just occasionally, or when some emergency arises, but continually."

THE VARIOUS MODERN TRANSLATIONS

The first step toward serious study of the Bible is to obtain a translation which you can understand.

The King James Version, translated in 1611 A.D., has never been rivaled for poetic beauty and majesty of expression. From a purely literary viewpoint, it towers over all modern translations as a Shakespeare play does over a TV western.

But more than a thousand English words and phrases used in the Bible have undergone significant changes of meaning since the King James was published more than three and a half centuries ago. Furthermore, modern scholarship, abetted by archaeological discoveries and documentary finds, has cast valuable new light on many hitherto obscure passages of the Old Testament (which was originally written in Hebrew) and the New Testament (written in Greek).

Modern translations take advantage of these new insights into the original meaning of the Scripture. And they use contemporary English instead of seventeenth-century English.

Which modern translation you choose is a matter of taste. The chief contenders for public and scholarly favor are the Revised Standard Version and the New English Bible. You will find samples of both of these in this book.*

The Revised Standard Version was prepared by a team of American scholars. It is essentially a rewrite and updating of the old King James, using the same sentence structures but substituting contemporary for archaic English words where necessary for clarity.

The New English Bible is the work of a team of British scholars. It is an entirely fresh translation from the original Hebrew and Greek into modern, idiomatic English. While it lacks literary grace at many points, it hits the reader right between the eyes as a message addressed to him in his own everyday tongue. Those who have ceased to get any real impact out of overly familiar passages of the King James Version will have the feeling that they are reading the Bible for the first time.

* Turn to the end of Chapter 10 where, under "Three texts you may want to reread," The Ten Commandments and the Parable of the Good Samaritan are reprinted from the Revised Standard Version. Jesus' description of The Last Judgment is from the New English Bible.

Where you begin reading is just as important as the choice of a translation. Many people make the mistake of trying to read the Bible straight through from beginning to end, as if it were an ordinary book. If you do that, you are very apt to get "bogged down in the begats" when you reach the dull and endless genealogies of the Old Testament.

It is more accurate to think of the Bible as a whole library of books, written at various times over a span of two thousand years. These books differ enormously in literary style, historical value, and spiritual depth. Except in a very broad sense, they do not tell a consecutive narrative, so there's no need to begin at the beginning and plow straight through.

Instead, you can begin in the middle, with the part of the Bible which to Christians is the most important and exciting news ever reported upon this earth—the story of Jesus Christ.

"The Bible is a book about God; it tells what he did for men, especially in Jesus Christ His son," says Professor Floyd V. Filson of McCormick Theological Seminary. "Read the whole Bible by all means, but get to the heart of the Biblical message at the start."

TRY TO READ ST. LUKE'S GOSPEL FIRST

An excellent place to begin is with the New Testament books of Luke and Acts. They were written by the same author, and although they are now separated in the Bible, it is clear that they were originally intended to go together, for they tell a single, connected story.

The first part—the Gospel according to St. Luke—is the

story of Christ's life, death, and Resurrection, written especially for a Gentile audience by a man who seems to have been a very careful reporter with an eye for vivid detail and a gift for poetic expression.

In the Acts of the Apostles, the same writer tells how the Christian Church came into being under the awesome impact of the Resurrection, and traces its spread throughout the Roman Empire, with particular attention to the missionary voyages of the Apostle Paul, with whom Luke traveled extensively.

After reading Luke and Acts, you may want to proceed to the Gospel according to St. John. Here you'll find less concern with events and sayings, more emphasis on meaning and significance. To oversimplify, you might say that Luke is the reporter who tells you what Jesus did and said, while John is the theologian who tells who Jesus was and why he came.

St. Paul's letters could well come next—especially those addressed to the young churches at Corinth and Rome. After that you can finish the other Gospels and Epistles of the New Testament in almost any order that appeals to you.

Easing your way into the Old Testament

Eventually, you'll want to read the whole Old Testament, for Christianity cannot be truly comprehended without a thorough acquaintance with the Jewish Scriptures which Jesus said he came "not to destroy but to fulfill."

But it may be best to ease your way into the Old Testament by reading first the Book of Psalms—the greatest collection of devotional poetry the world has ever known.

After the Psalms, try Isaiah, the noblest and most moving of the Hebrew books of "prophecy." Then, when you're well acquainted with the sublime heights to which the children of Israel are destined to move in their knowledge of God, you can go back to Genesis and begin tracing the early story of this remarkable people who were chosen by God for a special role as light-bearers to mankind.

In the early books of the Old Testament, you will find a fascinating variety of material. Along with authentic history of the Jewish people, there are myths and folklore. Great moral laws which have formed the conscience of western civilization are intermingled with detailed regulations for the observances of ancient feasts and ceremonies. There are vivid biographies of great heroes like Moses, great scoundrels like Haman, noble women like Ruth, wanton sluts like Jezebel, and complex personalities like David who were capable of being very good and very wicked. There are wise and witty epigrams in the Book of Proverbs, and the Song of Solomon is an erotic love poem which would get any book other than the Bible banned in Boston.

You'll find dull stretches in the Bible, as you will in any other book. With a little practice, however, you can soon learn how to skim quickly over the specifications for the Temple at Jerusalem, or the account of an ancient battle, to light upon the gems of prose and poetry which are scattered through every part of the Bible, even such difficult-to-read books as Leviticus and Revelations.

A GOOD COMMENTARY WILL HELP

Whatever sequence you follow, you will find far more meaning in the Bible if you read it in connection with a good commentary. Before beginning to read any book of the Bible, find out from the commentary what scholars have discovered about its date and authorship, and the historical circumstances under which it was written. This background information will enable you to understand many otherwise baffling passages.

Even with the help of a commentary, you'll encounter many things in the Bible which will puzzle you, and which may seem contrary to the spirit of Christ. When that happens, mark the passage for further exploration, in another commentary or in conversation with a more experienced Bible student. But don't let it upset you. Most of the great heresies of Christianity, from the first century to the present, have resulted from reading too much into an ambiguous passage of Scripture. Any single verse of the Bible, taken in isolation, may actually be dangerous to your spiritual health. Every part of it must be read in relation to the whole message. And the ultimate criterion by which all of the Bible is to be interpreted is Jesus Christ, the living Word of God.

5

ACCEPTING THE MIRACLES

"Am I really expected to swallow all of those miracle stories in the Bible?"

The woman who blurted out that question at an adult confirmation class was not really the lonely heretic she thought herself to be. Millions of church members today, including not a few clergymen and theologians, share her tendency to gag on the miracles recorded in the Bible. If there is one article of faith to which the modern intellectual is firmly committed, it is the proposition that "miracles can't happen."

Unwilling to let go of Christ, and unable to accept the reality of the miraculous events which the New Testament associates with him, liberal theologians of the nineteenth century tried to extract from the Gospels a miracle-free Christianity which would not offend the "scientific" mind. But what they had left when they got through with the process of reduction was hardly worth arguing about. They had thrown out the baby with the bath water, and if "liberal" Christianity didn't provoke many attacks from skeptics, neither did it excite much devotion.

WHAT IS DE-MYTHOLOGIZING?

Although liberal theology has been passé for a long time, its effort to denature the Gospel has been taken up in recent years by the disciples of German theologian Rudolf Bultmann. Bultmann contends that the saving Word which God spoke through Christ can be communicated to modern man only by "de-mythologizing" the New Testament (i.e., stripping away its supernatural elements).

The trouble is, it won't work. The Christian Church was founded, and the New Testament was written, by men who were totally convinced that they had witnessed a mighty sign from God. The first disciples concluded that "Jesus is Lord"—the original and still most basic Christian creed—not because they were attracted to his moral teachings, but because they had seen him raised from the dead. And the early Church never hesitated to rest its whole case on the actual historicity of the Resurrection. "If Christ be not risen," St. Paul said, "then our faith is in vain."

While the Resurrection is the supreme miracle on which the whole New Testament rests, every page of the Gospels contains accounts of other strange and wondrous happenings which attended the earthly ministry of Jesus Christ. Men and women by the hundreds were healed by his touch —healed not only of ailments which might have been psychosomatic, but also of leprosy, tuberculosis, and congenital deformities. The world of nature seemed to respond to his wishes as a matter of course, so that bread multiplied in his hands as he passed it out to the hungry, and a raging storm stilled at the sound of his voice.

Anyone who reads the Gospels with an open mind finds himself pushed relentlessly toward the choice which St. Paul bluntly outlined: either these things really happened, however improbable they may sound; or the New Testament is a patchwork of lies, and Christianity is a fraudulent fairy story to which no one should give the least credence.

A person can honestly choose either of these alternatives. But no one should embrace the second of them in the naïve belief that modern science has "proved" that miracles are "impossible."

An incredibly large number of otherwise intelligent people entertain this notion. Actually, the one thing which no reputable scientist would ever claim to have proved is a negative. Science can and does say that certain things have happened with such regularity in the past that it is reasonable to expect that they will happen in the same way in the future. But the "laws" of nature discovered by science are really statements of overwhelming probability, rather than immutable definitions of what inexorably *must* be. There is no such word as "impossible" in the lexicon of genuine science.

PART OF THE TROUBLE STEMS FROM SEMANTICS

Part of the difficulty which many people have with the idea of miracles stems from semantics. They define a miracle as an occurrence "contrary to the laws of nature." Aside from the fact that this definition smuggles in the spurious concept of "laws" discussed in the previous paragraph, it also manages to convey the impression that a miracle is unnatural. St. Augustine dealt with this more than a thousand years ago. "A miracle is not contrary to nature, but to what is known of nature," he said. "We do not say that God does something contrary to nature because He acts in a way that is contrary to our knowledge of nature."

St. Augustine put the emphasis where it needs to be placed: a miracle is an act of God which attracts our attention, or even stirs our awe, because it differs from the way in which God usually does things.

In a profound sense, it would be no more miraculous for water to run uphill than it is for it to run downhill. We are accustomed to see it run downhill, and have postulated a force called gravity to explain why it does. But the "law" of gravity, like everything else in the created universe, exists solely because it is the will of God that it should exist.

Our experience (including the special kind of experience called science) tells us that God usually—indeed, nearly always—wills His universe to operate in an orderly and predictable manner which enables man to anticipate the results of certain actions, and to speak confidently of causes and effects. But there is nothing in science, theology, or logic which justifies the belief that God is a prisoner of the regularities and rhythms which man has observed in the order of nature. If He wants to intervene in the world He has created, to suspend the normal pattern of cause and effect and to bring about an atypical event which startled human observers call a "miracle," it is sheer absurdity to say that He *cannot* do so.

While acknowledging that "all things are possible unto God," some sincere people continue to balk at miracles on the grounds that the Great Designer of nature would not "capriciously" tamper with the orderly processes He has set in motion. The implication is that it is beneath God's dignity to put His oar into the affairs of human creatures on one small planet.

WERE MIRACLES GOD'S SIGNS?

The Bible thoroughly agrees with this view. Although Biblical writers did not know as well as we that our Earth is a speck of dust in the vast reaches of the cosmos, they were perhaps more mindful than we of the great condescension of God in taking any notice whatever of the puny creature who calls himself Man.

They believed that God cared about man—not because this seemed a right and proper thing for God to do—but rather because the evidence of His loving concern was irresistibly borne in on them. They saw God's hand particularly in certain unusual acts called miracles, but never regarded these acts as "capricious" interventions. On the contrary, they always looked upon miracles as "signs"—means by which God communicated with men, and revealed Himself to them.

This attitude toward miracles is especially evident in the New Testament, where virtually all of the miracles attributed to Jesus are directly associated with some lesson he was trying to teach or some insight he wanted to give to his disciples. Thus, from the Biblical viewpoint, the real question to be asked about any miracle is not how it happened but why: what was God saying to us in this *significant* act?

For those who believe that God revealed Himself uniquely and supremely in the person of Christ, it does not seem surprising that his career on earth was attended by many "miraculous" events designed to open the eyes and hearts of men. Once we have accepted the great central miracles of the Incarnation and the Resurrection, we have no good reason for rejecting out of hand the incidental miracles recorded in the New Testament.

On the other hand, belief in the possibility of miracles does not necessarily entail automatic acceptance of the historicity of every marvelous event reported by pious folk, in the Bible or elsewhere. Many of the "miracles" of the Old Testament, such as the story of the whale swallowing Jonah, can be regarded in the same light as Jesus' parables: they are stories designed to teach a moral lesson, and whether "it really happened" is no more germane to the story of Jonah than to Jesus' immortal story of the Prodigal Son.

Even in the New Testament, whose essential historicity has been strongly vindicated by modern scholarship, we cannot be certain that any particular minor event actually took place just as it has been recorded. Biblical criticism, in authenticating the main outlines of the Gospel story, has also taught us that there are several literary forms besides straight historical narrative in the New Testament. The beloved nativity stories, for example, contain family reminiscences which may well have undergone a certain amount of dramatization, just like the stories handed down in your family.

The Question of the Virgin Birth

Of all the miracles associated with the life of Christ, none seems to be a greater stumbling block for moderns than the Virgin Birth. Every now and then some bishop or clergyman will reap a harvest of headlines by declaring that he doesn't believe in it. Conservatives truculently defend it as one of the "fundamentals" of Christian faith.

I must confess here that I find this whole angry argument rather absurd. If fundamentalists are right in contending that no one can be a Christian without believing that Jesus was born of a Virgin, it seems very strange that the doctrine is not even mentioned in two of the Gospels (Mark and John). And St. Paul, who wrote over half of the New Testament, does not once refer to it.

On the other hand, liberals are certainly illogical when they accept the miracle of the Resurrection but boggle at the notion that God could cause a baby to be conceived without the agency of a human father.

The one plain fact about the story of the Virgin Birth, on which everyone should be able to agree, is that it has served for nearly twenty centuries as a highly effective way of saying that Christ was both truly human and truly divine.

Since the Virgin Birth has proved to be the best way of expressing the truth of the Incarnation (which is acknowledged even by those who regard it as a legend), I can see no reason for questioning its historical validity. Why should God resort to a legend to communicate a truth which He was free to express in an actual event?

Do miracles still happen?

As a wire-service reporter steeped in the skepticism of my craft, I am personally quite certain that miracles still do happen. I am satisfied that I have witnessed extraordinary acts of God in my own life and in the lives of others whom I know extremely well. But it would be futile to recount the circumstances of these events. Every one of them can be "explained" by anyone endowed with unlimited faith in the twin gods of naturalism, chance and coincidence.

It is a documentable fact, however, that belief in miracles, especially miracles of healing, has undergone a widespread renascence in the Christian community during the past few years. Spiritual healing services, remarkably like those described in the Acts of the Apostles, are being held today in hundreds of churches affiliated with main-line Protestant denominations. Because there has been and still is so much charlatanism in this field, these churches carefully avoid any sensational publicity for inexplicable cures. But such cures are taking place in ordinary American churches in ordinary cities like Philadelphia and Washington, D. C., just as they have taken place for many years, under the most rigorous medical scrutiny, at the Roman Catholic shrine of Lourdes in France.

THE KIND OF FAITH THAT MATTERS

In 1961, I was privileged to have a long private talk with a gentle, serene Englishwoman named Dorothy Kerin, who has played a leading part in the revival of a spiritual healing ministry in the Anglican Communion and other major non-Roman churches.

Miss Kerin told me in a very matter-of-fact way about the experience which convinced her that "the Lord Jesus still walks among us . . . and what he did in Galilee two thousand years ago, he can and does do now."

"It happened fifty years ago, when I was a young girl," she said. "I had been bedridden for several years with advanced tuberculosis. My body had wasted away. For nearly a week I had been blind and deaf, and my doctors expected me to die at any moment. It was then that I had the vision . . . or whatever you want to call it.

"I was in a place of exquisite beauty and suddenly beheld a figure in white coming towards me. I ran to meet him. 'No, Dorothy,' he said. 'You're not coming yet. Will you go back and do something for me?'

"I answered, 'Yes, Lord,' and then I opened my eyes and saw people standing about my bed. I cried out to them, 'Did you not hear? I am well, I must get up and walk.' And I did."

From that moment, she said, every symptom of her illness disappeared and she quickly regained normal weight.

He had said "Do something for me." But what? For several years she did not know. "I had to learn," she explained, "that waiting patiently is one form of obedience."

It was only after she had become an adult that she understood her mission. She talked to church authorities, eventually to the Archbishop of Canterbury. Under his spiritual sponsorship, she began to lay her hands on sick people, and pray for their healing. Not all of them recovered; but some did, in a way that physicians could not explain.

In recent years, she has carried on her ministry in a Home of Healing at Burrswood, England. It is a state-registered nursing home, with a trained medical staff. Miss Kerin always has insisted that prayer is "not a substitute, but a reinforcement" for medical science. Near the hospital is a chapel, The Church of Christ the Healer, where healing services are held as an integral part of divine worship according to the liturgy of the Church of England.

Unlike many so-called faith healers, Miss Kerin does not demand that sick people "believe" they will be healed. On the contrary, she emphasizes at every service that Jesus himself got no for an answer when he prayed that the cup of suffering might pass from him.

"It is not 'expectation' but acceptance of God's will that is important," she said. "Obedience is the key that unlocks the door to every profound spiritual experience."

Why do healing miracles seem to be granted to some people, but not to others?

"I do not know why God acts as he does in any particular case. And I do not try to rationalize the paradox that some get well while others do not. I know only that we find the same paradox in the New Testament, and throughout Christian experience. Some of God's greatest saints have not been made whole physically. But they have been given the grace to triumph gloriously over their afflictions.

"I don't think you can make any water-tight theory to explain all that happens—and doesn't happen. As the Bible says, the spirit 'bloweth where it wisteth.'

"The kind of faith that matters is not an assurance that your prayers will be answered just so. It is the kind Luther talked about—'a lively, reckless confidence in the grace of God.' With that you can face anything."

6

LEARNING TO PRAY

"The Lord is near; have no anxiety, but in every-thing make your requests known to God in prayer and peti-tion with thanksgiving. Then the peace of God, which is beyond our utmost understanding, will keep guard over your hearts and thoughts, in Christ Jesus."

St. Paul gave that advice to the Christians at Philippi in a letter written from his prison cell in Rome about 64 A.D. The passage of nineteen centuries has not diminished its timeliness.

If there is one thing which distinguishes a real Christian from a mere church member, it is prayer. God remains a hypothesis until we get to know him, first hand, through prayer.

TALKING TO GOD

What is prayer? The childhood definition, "Prayer is talking to God," is adequate as a starting place. All of us begin by talking to God, or more realistically, talking *at*

God. Those who persist in the life of prayer come to realize, however, that it is a two-way communication, a conversation with God rather than a monologue.

These are not merely pious words. They are an attempt to describe, as simply and accurately as possible, an experience which has been shared by millions of Christians from the time of St. Paul until now. If you will accept their testimony as a sufficient reason for giving prayer an honest try, you can verify for yourself the extravagant claim that it is possible for a human being to enter into an intimate, I-Thou dialogue with the Infinite Ground of Being.

Before we take up the human side of prayer, let's try to deal with a question which must arise in the mind of any person who takes the foregoing paragraph seriously.

How does God speak to us in prayer?

Only a very few people, the true mystics, ever have the kind of experience described by Dorothy Kerin in the last chapter. God communicates with most of His human children through a "still, small voice"—the Quakers say a "light"—which dwells deep within a man and speaks to him as directly and wordlessly as his own conscience.

WHAT IS THE TRINITY?

In Christian theology, this inner voice is called the Holy Spirit. The very words "Holy Spirit" are enough to throw many church members for a loss, because they have come to associate them with the doctrine of the Trinity, which they find baffling and disturbing, an apparent contradiction of monotheism.

It may help to point out that the term "Trinity" appears nowhere in the New Testament. It is a word coined by theologians in the post-Apostolic era, when the necessities of evangelism made it necessary to express the Christian community's experience in verbal formulae and creeds.

The theologians tried to say in the doctrine of the Trinity that man can know God in three different ways: (1) as the transcendent, wholly other Being who created and sustains the universe (the Father); (2) as the Christ who entered history to rescue men from themselves (the Son); or (3) as an Indwelling Spirit who is closer to man than breathing (the Holy Spirit).

The New Testament has a great deal to say about the Holy Spirit. As Christ is the center of the Four Gospels, the Spirit is the dominant figure of the Acts of the Apostles. His presence was so vividly felt in the early Church that it was often accompanied by ecstatic reactions, such as "speaking in tongues." St. Paul thought that man could receive no greater gift than to be "filled with the Spirit." It is the Spirit, he declared, who prompts men to seek communion with God, who opens their eyes to the truths of faith, who bears witness within their hearts to the reality of God and the forgiveness of Christ, and who strengthens their limp wills to continue the ever uphill climb toward righteousness.

In the New Testament, and in Christian experience, the Holy Spirit is closely linked to prayer. It is through prayer that we open our minds and hearts and wills to the Spirit. This is what we mean by the ancient cliché, "draw nigh to God in prayer."

How can you learn to pray?

At this point, you may be thinking: "But I've tried to pray, and it doesn't seem to do any good. How can I learn to pray?"

It is a question which no one need be ashamed to ask.

The apostles asked it of Jesus, and he replied with some very specific advice on how to pray, including the model prayer which is recorded in the sixth chapter of St. Matthew's Gospel:

Our Father who art in heaven,
Hallowed be thy name.
Thy kingdom come.
Thy will be done,
    On earth as it is in heaven.
Give us this day our daily bread,
And forgive us our trespasses,
    As we forgive those who trespass against us.
Lead us not into temptation,
But deliver us from evil.
For thine is the kingdom, and the power, and the glory
    forever.

                                              Amen.

It is the most widely used prayer in the world today, by a considerable margin. Catholics know it as the "Our Father." Protestants usually call it the Lord's Prayer.

Throughout the ages, many saints and spiritual counselors have contributed other practical suggestions about prayer.

Some people are offended by the idea that there are rules to be learned and disciplines to be practiced in prayer. They may acknowledge a place for formal prayers in public worship, but they insist that private prayer should always be unstudied and unrehearsed, a spontaneous outpouring of the heart.

Let us hasten to agree that spontaneous prayer has great

value, and that it is appropriate for any time, place or circumstance. As the saintly old Scot, George Macdonald, said, "never wait for fitter time or place to talk to God . . . He will listen as thou walkest."

But if your devotional life is confined solely to spontaneous, spur-of-the-moment prayers—in other words, if you pray only when you "feel like it"—you will find your spirit starving of malnutrition.

THE FIRST RULE IS REGULARITY

The first rule laid down by the saints and sages for those who would truly draw nigh to God in prayer is *regularity*. Pray each day at the same time. No matter how many spontaneous prayers you may offer during the course of the day, you should also have a fixed time for private prayer. Treat it as the most important appointment of your day, and don't let anything intrude upon it or crowd it out. Some people pray best early in the morning, before they are involved in the day's activities. Others prefer to pray before retiring at night. The important thing is to pick a time you can call your own, and stick to it every day.

It is a good idea to have an habitual place, as well as a regular time, for prayer. It may be any place you find convenient, so long as it affords complete privacy. Jesus recommended a closet. In the modern home or apartment, that might be translated into a bedroom or bathroom. Lock the door if possible. Your ability to concentrate on your prayers is directly related to your assurance that no one will see, overhear or interrupt you.

The posture you assume in prayer does not matter to God, but it may make a great difference to you. You can stand, sit, kneel, or lie down to pray. Kneeling is a physical act of humility which helps many people to prepare psychologically for prayer. An uncomfortable position may be a distraction, but one which is too comfortable—for example, lying in bed—is likely to lead to drowsiness rather than concentration.

Many people find it helpful to prepare for prayer with a brief period of devotional reading. This helps you to make the transition from the hectic world of daily routine to the quiet mood of prayer. It enables you to focus your attention on God, which is both the precondition and the purpose of prayer. The Bible is the supreme devotional book. You can do no better than to begin your prayers by reading a psalm or a selection from the New Testament. Other classics of devotional literature include *The Confessions of St. Augustine* and *The Imitation of Christ*. Two of the best modern devotional books are *Daily Strength for Daily Needs* by Mary Wilder Tileston, and *A Diary of Readings* by John Baillie. There are many others.

Pray as long as you need to or want to—and no longer. Jesus warned that long-windedness is not a virtue in prayer, and the model prayer he gave to his disciples is only sixty-seven words long. Until you are far advanced in the spiritual life, you may find it difficult to sustain a genuine mood of prayer for longer than five or ten minutes at a stretch. It is better to pray briefly and regularly than to indulge in marathon prayers one day and then "skip" several days.

BE YOURSELF WHEN YOU PRAY

Another very important rule is cited by the Very Rev. John B. Coburn, dean of the Episcopal Theological

School, Cambridge, Massachusetts, in his excellent little book, *Prayer and Personal Religion*.

"Be yourself," the dean counsels. "Be natural before God. Do not pretend to emotions you do not feel. Tell him whatever is on your heart and mind with whatever words are most natural to you. You do not have to speak to Him in 'religious' language about 'spiritual' matters only . . .

"Speak as naturally and as easily as you would to a friend, since God is just that . . . This natural expression of yourself at the outset is the guarantee that you can go on to a creative, free and mature relationship with God."

A corollary to this advice is that you need not be ashamed to offer "selfish" prayers, or to seek God's help in "little" things. "Anything large enough for a wish to light upon, is large enough to hang a prayer on," says George Macdonald. Remember that Jesus included in his sample prayer a petition for bread, which is about as mundane a request as you can make. Since our "selfish" needs and everyday problems inevitably loom large in our minds, especially when we are first beginning to climb the ladder of prayer, it is simply hypocritical—a violation of Dean Coburn's injunction to absolute honesty—to try to ignore them in our prayers. Much better to lay them before God and get them out of the way.

PETITIONING GOD

Asking God for things—whether they be spiritual things such as grace, or worldly things such as daily bread—is *petitionary prayer*. It has the great value of helping to establish a personal, Father-child relationship with God. The Bible teaches, and Christian experience confirms, that God always hears and sometimes grants our petitions. But petitionary prayer is not a kind of magic incantation by which man can make God jump through hoops. The words which distinguish truly Christian petitions are those which Jesus spoke in the Garden of Gethsemane, as he faced, in a very human agony of dread, the ordeal of the crucifixion.

"Father," he prayed, "all things are possible to Thee. Take this cup away from me.

"Nevertheless, not my will but Thine be done."

That "nevertheless" is not easy to say sincerely. But when it is truly said, it transforms the whole prayer. The petitioner begins by asking for something he desperately wants, and ends by accepting whatever Infinite Goodness knows to be right and necessary and best—even if it be a cross.

The prayer which culminates in "Thy will be done" does not presume that God needs to be told what to do. It does not presume that He can be wheedled into granting special favors for those who clamorously appeal to him. It presumes only that He is the kind of Father who wants His children to flee to Him when they are in trouble, and whose arms are always open, particularly when He has to say no.

INTERCESSION AND CONFESSION

Intercession has been described as "loving your neighbor on your knees." It is the prayer in which we seek God's help for other people. It is important to avoid vague and meaningless generalities ("please bless the poor and sick") and to pray for the specific needs of specific individuals. Some people feel that it is unnecessary and even presumptuous to call God's attention to problems which He surely knows about, or to seek His blessing for people whom He already loves more than we can. But Jesus explicitly taught us to pray for others, including those who hate, despise, and mistreat us. Christians who have practiced intercessory prayer are absolutely certain of its efficacy. It goes without saying that intercessory prayers, like petitionary prayers, should always be offered with the Great Nevertheless: "not my will, but thine be done."

Confession is the prayer in which we acknowledge our sins and accept God's forgiveness of them. Here again, it is better to be specific whenever possible, remembering however that we have doubtless offended in many ways that we do not recognize. In confession, we humbly and contritely admit that we have become separated from God by our own sinfulness, and we open our lives to healing, reconciling, restoring, uplifting grace of Him who loves us in spite of what we are.

COUNT YOUR BLESSINGS

Thanksgiving means counting your blessings. As in the case of intercession and confession, it is always better to be specific—to thank God sincerely for particular good things in your life. The true spirit of thanksgiving also accepts the adversities of life, and sees even in them the merciful if sometimes mysterious hand of a Loving Father.

Adoration is the highest form of prayer. It means lifting up your heart to God and saying in whatever words you find most meaningful that you acknowledge Him to be worthy of your utmost love and obedience. The Lord's Prayer begins with a simple expression of adoration: "Our Father which art in heaven, hallowed by thy name, thy kingdom come, thy will be done . . ." There are many other beautiful and majestic prayers of adoration in the Psalms and in other prayer books of more recent vintage.

There is nothing wrong with using a prayer composed by

someone else, so long as you really *pray it* instead of passively reading it. People who pray regularly often find their own prayers falling into a monotonous rut. A good prayer book will suggest topics of prayer and meditation which you may not have thought of on your own. It can be particularly useful in widening the horizons of your prayers of thanksgiving and adoration.

But don't consult a prayer book just to find more elegant words for what you have to say to God. He will hear what is in your heart, not what is on your lips. There is no prayer of thanksgiving half so eloquent as a moment of genuine gratitude. And no prayer of adoration will ever soar higher than a pure heart's simple cry:

"I love you, God."

7

THE REASONS FOR GOING TO CHURCH

If I read the Bible, and pray regularly at home, and try to live a good Christian life all through the week, is it really so important that I go to church on Sunday morning?

Unfortunately for all of us who like to sleep late on Sundays, the straight answer to that question is a simple yes. It *is* important to go to church on Sunday—in fact, to form the habit of going *every* Sunday.

It doesn't matter whether the preacher is mediocre, and his sermons bore you to tears. It doesn't matter whether the guy in the next pew is a fearful hypocrite who prays loudly on Sunday and cheats his fellow man on Monday. It doesn't even matter whether the service drags on too long and leaves you feeling irritated and impatient rather than basking in a warm glow of piety.

The real reason for participating in public worship is that it is, like private prayer, a time-tested and dependable means of "drawing nigh unto God." If you go to church expecting to meet God there, you will not be disappointed.

He can and will speak to you through the dullest sermon, or the worst-sung hymn, if you are genuinely listening for *His* voice.

Although God approaches us in many different kinds of corporate worship, it has been the experience of the Christian community for twenty centuries that He is particularly accessible in the ancient rite known variously as Holy Communion, the Lord's Supper, the Eucharist, or the Mass.

This central and supreme act of Christian worship was instituted by Christ himself at his last supper with his disciples, in the upper room of a house in Jerusalem, a few hours before he was arrested, tried, and crucified.

THE SACRED MYSTERY OF COMMUNION

The earliest written account of the simple ritual he performed, and the meaning he gave to it, is found in St. Paul's First Epistle to the Corinthians.

". . . The Lord Jesus in the night in which he was betrayed took bread; and when he had given thanks, he brake it, and said, 'This is my body, which is broken for you: this do in remembrance of me.' In like manner also the cup, after supper, saying, 'This cup is the new covenant in my blood: this do, as oft as ye drink it, in remembrance of me.'"

Thus bread and wine were perpetually associated, for Christians, with the body and blood of Christ which were sacrificed to redeem men from their sins.

Eucharist, from a Greek word meaning thanksgiving, seems to have been the earliest term applied to the service. Ancient records show that regular celebration of the Eucharist began in the primitive Christian church early in the first century A.D. It has continued ever since in virtually all branches of Christendom (the Quakers being the most notable exception).

Although Christians are united in their fidelity to this act of worship, they differ in their understanding of its nature and significance.

Some Protestants—for example, Baptists, Disciples of Christ, and Pentecostal groups—observe the Lord's Supper as a "memorial" service. They believe that its primary purpose is to remind Christians that "while we were yet sinners, Christ died for us." It also serves as a "fellowship meal," emphasizing the ties of love that bind Christians.

The vast majority of Christians in the world—including Roman Catholics, Eastern Orthodox, Anglicans, Lutherans, Presbyterians, and Methodists—regard the Eucharist as much more than that. They call it a "sacrament," or sacred mystery. They hold that God acts through the sacrament in a supernatural way to impart to believers the uplifting of mind, the purifying of motive and the strengthening of will that is called grace.

The sacramental churches differ mainly in defining the nature of the eucharistic miracle. Roman Catholic and Eastern Orthodox churches teach that the elements of the service, while retaining the external appearance of bread and wine, are literally changed (in Catholic terminology, "transubstantiated") into the body and blood of Christ at the moment of consecration. These communions regard the celebration of the Mass as a "renewal" or "re-enactment" of Christ's sacrifice on the Cross.

Leaders of the Protestant Reformation rejected the doctrine of transubstantiation and sought to eliminate from the Mass any suggestion of a "repetition" of the atoning act of Christ which, they said, was performed once and for all on Calvary.

While asserting that the bread and wine of Communion are sacred symbols rather than the literal body and blood of Christ, the Reformation churches held—and still hold —that Christ is spiritually "present" in the Eucharist in a real and unique sense. They believe that those who partake of the sacrament truly partake of Christ, receiving his spirit as nourishment for their souls.

Whether you take a "high" or "low" view of the Eucharist, it is worth bearing in mind that this is the only act of public worship which was specifically ordained by Christ. Exactly how and why it serves as a channel of grace may be open to theological debate. But the overwhelming testimony of practicing Christians in every generation since the Apostles has been that *it does work*. For His own good reasons (which are rarely very clear or plausible-sounding to men) God has seen fit to use this particular rite as an open circuit between time and eternity.

THE MEANING OF BAPTISM

There is one other sacrament which is observed in all major Christian bodies, and which can be traced back to Jesus himself. It is known universally as baptism, and although the various churches have different ideas about how and when it should be administered, they are united in the conviction that *something tremendously important happens to a human being when he is baptized*.

A good many people today, including some clergymen who ought to know better, seem to look upon baptism as a sort of initiation rite by which a person becomes a member of the Church. But this fraternity-house or lodge-hall view of baptism is a travesty of true Christian doctrine.

The doctrine is admittedly not easy to explain. Like everything else that approaches the live core of the man-God relationship, it is wrapped in mystery. If we speak carelessly of what happens in baptism, we make the whole thing sound like black magic, and repel honest intellectuals. But if we shy too far away from the mystery, we fail to do justice to baptism, or to make clear why Christians think it so desirable that everyone be baptized.

One traditional way of describing what happens in baptism is to say that a person is "born again." His first birth was physical, and made him a member of a human family. The second birth in baptism is spiritual, and makes him a member of the Christian family, a child of God, an Inheritor of the Kingdom of Heaven.

A more helpful approach, for some people, is through St. Paul's metaphorical description of the Church as "the Body of Christ." It is necessary to bear in mind that St. Paul used the metaphor in an exceedingly literal sense. He was saying that Christians are meant to be the hands and feet, the arms and legs, the eyes and ears of Christ, now that He is no longer physically present in the world. Baptism is the act—and it is always an act of God, not of the officiating minister—by which a person is *engrafted* into this living organism, and made, in the good old phrase of the Book of Common Prayer, a "very member incorporate of the mystical body of Christ."

The thing to remember about both of these descriptions of baptism, and any others you may encounter, is that they are human attempts to verbalize something which the Christian community has experienced and therefore believes deeply, even though it doesn't understand it very well. What was said of Holy Communion must be said again of baptism: for His own good and impenetrable reasons, God has chosen this rite as a vehicle for conferring his grace upon men and transforming their innermost beings to such a radical degree that they can be said to have been born anew.

The sacraments of baptism and Holy Communion are not the only means by which a human person may be reborn and sustained as a child of God. Even the Roman Catholic Church, which long seemed to recognize no salvation outside its own fold, now teaches that God's grace overflows all institutional channels and continually confounds those who would restrict its operation to any particular sphere. But if you were looking for a man who was widely and reliably reported to live in Cleveland, you would be exceedingly foolish to conduct your search in Seattle, on the chance that he *might* drop in there some day on a visit. It is in the Church, and through the sacraments, that men have found Christ for twenty centuries, and those who sincerely seek him will look for him there.

8

THE ENIGMA OF EVIL AND SUFFERING

Clergymen call it "The Great Why" and it is the hardest question they encounter in their pastoral ministry. *"Why did God let this happen?"*

"This" may be the death of a child . . . the lingering agony of a cancer patient . . . the capricious destruction of a natural disaster . . . the mute suffering of an animal . . . or any other tragedy which stirs compassion or self-pity.

Inability to find a satisfactory answer to The Great Why is probably the chief cause of religious doubt. Many people have become practical if not professing atheists because they cannot believe that a just and loving God could have created a world in which there is so much pain and evil.

When a person's faith founders on the fact of evil, he is likely to think that he has discovered an argument against God which has never occurred to those who believe in Him.

But this is not true.

Believers in God have wrestled with the problem of evil for thousands of years. No modern writer could state the enigma of undeserved suffering more forcefully than it is stated in the Old Testament book of Job. And no cynic could express the dilemma more candidly than it has been expressed by such Christian theologians as St. Augustine, C. S. Lewis, and Austin Farrer.

THE CASE AGAINST GOD

Following their good example, let's lay out the case against God in the strongest possible terms.

If God were all-powerful and all-loving, as Christians believe, He presumably could have created a world in which everything would have proceeded harmoniously and all of His creatures would have been safe and happy.

Instead, we find ourselves and our fellow creatures, the animals, struggling for survival in a violent universe where physical accidents occur with wanton unpredictability, where nature is "red of fang and claw," where human beings increase their own misery by deliberate acts of cruelty toward one another, where all life is beset by many uncertainties and bounded with one great certainty—the certainty of death.

"If we face the facts honestly," the skeptic asks, "must we not conclude that the Power which set this universe in motion is entirely indifferent to the fate of the creatures that chance to inhabit it?"

The short answer is, no. By all means let's face the facts honestly, but let's face *all* of them, not just the ones which seem to militate against belief in God.

This world, for all of its troubles, is by no means as bleak as people are wont to depict it when they are pumping up the problem of evil. The truth is that for most of us, most of the time, the blessings outweigh the banes of existence. That's why we cling so stubbornly to life.

It is true that we find ugliness, falsehood, evil, and hatred in our world. But we also encounter beauty, truth, goodness, and love. And it is much more difficult to explain how the latter could have evolved in a universe composed solely of brute matter than it is to conceive of reasons why a God of Love might have found it necessary to create the kind of world in which pain and evil could appear.

We can't assign motives to God

The reasons we conceive may not be the right ones, of course. That point should always be emphasized in dealing with any question about God which begins with "why." We can speak with some assurance about *what* God does, and *how* He seems to act under various circumstances. But we are treading on very dangerous ground when we begin glibly to assign motives to God. The assumption always implied in such speculation is that our finite minds can see things in the same light as Infinite Wisdom. This is an incredibly arrogant assumption. Humility aside, common sense should impel us to recognize the truth of the ancient Hebrew poet's admonition that the thoughts of God are "unsearchable" by man, and "his ways past finding out." A man from the Stone Age who watched an astronaut donning his space gear would be completely at a loss to comprehend the reason behind any step in the process. Yet the gulf of knowledge and understanding which separates stone age man and astronaut is miniscule compared to that which lies between human and Divine wisdom.

While we dare not claim to know for sure why God lets

"bad" things happen, it is not really necessary to explain each and every instance of pain and evil in the universe in order to explode the widely held notion that the existence of evil "disproves" the existence of God.

If we have other grounds for believing in God and trusting in his love—and I have tried to make clear in previous chapters that there are such grounds which millions of Christians find absolutely convincing—then it will be enough to satisfy ourselves that pain and evil *could* play a necessary role in the beneficent purposes of a Creator who wills for His human children a higher destiny than the "happiness" they are apt to seek for themselves.

Many will boggle at the word "necessary" in the preceding sentence, because they feel that any talk about God's being bound by inherent necessities contradicts the idea that he is omnipotent.

But, as the late C. S. Lewis pointed out, some things are impossible even to God because they are inherently contradictory. Thus it would be absurd to say that God can be entirely good and entirely evil at the same time.

Lewis said that God was confronted with two necessities when he chose to create human beings with free wills.

Rain Must Fall on the Just and Unjust

First, He had to give them an environment—the physical universe—in which to exist and make their choices. And if their choices were to have any real meaning, this environment must be neutral and stable, conferring its benefits and banes in accordance with impersonal and relatively inexorable natural laws. God may intervene to suspend these laws on rare occasions called miracles. But the rain must usually fall on the just and the unjust alike for the good reason that if it didn't, nature wouldn't be a neutral medium and human beings would become puppets instead of free souls.

Second, God had to accept the possibility that men would abuse their freedom, revolt against Him and His moral laws, and bring suffering on themselves and others.

Lewis asserted that these two factors—physical accident and human sinfulness—are the chief causes of the world's pain, and that both are indirect but inescapable consequences of the Divine will to create free human spirits.

Professor Austin Farrer of Oxford University develops a similar argument in his profound but readable book, *Love Almighty and Ills Unlimited*. He shows that a very large proportion of the suffering endured by human beings and all other sentient creatures results from the "mutual interference of systems" which is a necessary characteristic of a physical universe governed by natural laws.

"If God was pleased to create a physical universe, He was sure to set going an infinity of forces and a plurality of systems, mostly devoid of intelligence, and acting upon one another in accordance with the limited principles incorporated in each," says Professor Farrer. "Such a universe must inflict much accidental damage on the systems it contains; a damage which is the essential form of physical evil."

THE PRICE OF HUMAN FREEDOM

As for the non-physical or spiritual evil which abounds in the world, Professor Farrer agrees with C. S. Lewis that it is the price which God had to pay for giving human beings the freedom of choice which distinguishes them from brute beasts. Without free will, man would not be created "in the image of God." With it, he has the power to defy God's wishes and to bring misery on himself and others.

Many people are particularly distressed by animal pain, and consider the sufferings of dumb creatures to be the most telling of all arguments against belief in a benign Providence.

It must be admitted that animal pain cannot be attributed to a misuse of free will. We can say, however, that pain serves an indispensable role in helping to guide animals away from courses of conduct prejudicial to their survival, and into actions which are conducive to their well-being. We can also say that human sentimentality may greatly exaggerate the "suffering" of lower forms of life, by falsely imagining that their physical pains are accompanied by the same fears, anxieties, and other forms of psychic trauma that human beings experience. Beyond these observations, we can comprehend animal pain only as a function of the "clash of systems" which Professor Farrer holds to be inevitable in a physical universe.

SUFFERING DOESN'T ALWAYS ENNOBLE

When we focus our attention on human beings—the only creatures about whose suffering we have reliable first-hand knowledge—we find that there are several more things which can be said, which help to fit the "problem of evil" into a Christian perspective.

Pain and trouble can serve the incalculably valuable purpose of drawing us away from complacent preoccupation with the transitory pleasures of this world. They drive us to seek God by making us aware what weak and helpless creatures we really are, and how contingent are all of our hopes and plans. As C. S. Lewis said, "God whispers to us in our pleasures, speaks in our conscience, but shouts in our pains: it is his megaphone to rouse a deaf world."

Suffering does not always "ennoble" the human spirit. It sometimes makes people become more self-centered, mean, and hateful than ever. But Christian experience is illuminated by countless demonstrations that suffering *can* refine the human spirit, and lift it to sublime heights. What makes the difference is how we *accept* the hurts and disappointments and tragedies which befall us. If we wish, we can treat each of them as a sheer disaster, and mope over how "unfair" it is that this should have happened to us. Or we can accept our sorrows as Christ accepted his, praying for deliverance, but adding: "not my will but thine be done." When we accept our suffering—whether it results from physical accident, our own sins, or wrongs done to us by another—we are in effect offering it up to God as a willing sacrifice. And any practicing Christian can testify that God *always* contrives to bring good out of any suffering that is genuinely offered to Him. It sometimes takes a very long while to see where His hand was at work in what seemed at the time like an unmitigated tragedy. But no one who has really trusted Him has ever been let down.

Of course, the good which God brings out of the apparent evil of human suffering may be *spiritual good*, rather than a mere restoration of physical health or material prosperity. And skeptics will say that spiritual good is a poor recompense for bodily pain.

They may be right—if man's only destiny is the grave. All Christian answers to the problem of evil are based ultimately on the conviction that life in this world of trials and tribulations is meant to prepare men for eternity.

Skeptics will snort that this is "pie in the sky." But as Professor Farrer points out, there is really "no other consolation but this which carries any force." The issue is clearly drawn: either we believe in the Christian promise of eternal life, or we do not.

If the promise is false, man is indeed a cruel joke, a sentient bit of matter who has somehow evolved in a mindless universe, taunted by intimations of immortality but doomed to a brief and precarious existence, punctuated by pain and terminated by death.

But if the promise is true, man can accept whatever life brings with the assurance that "the sufferings of this present time are not worthy to be compared with the glory that shall be revealed in us as the children of God."

9

WILL THERE BE LIFE AFTER DEATH?

What happens when we die?

Man is the only creature who asks that question. But he asks it very insistently. It has bothered him since the dawn of human history. It is perhaps the most basic question he asks of any religion or philosophy which professes to help him comprehend the meaning of his existence.

There are four possible answers, and each of them has many adherents.

One theory is that death is the end of the line for human beings, as for other organisms. Life simply ceases to exist, and the indefinable essence which constitutes a human personality is swallowed up by nothingness. This is what secular humanists believe. It is not a "modern" idea. It is one of the oldest, if not *the* oldest, of all human guesses about death.

Also of great antiquity is the belief that man has a "soul" which *by its very nature* is imperishable. At death, this immortal part of man is separated from the physical body which suffers corruption. This is what the great Greek philosophers taught, and their view is held in our own day by many who mistakenly regard it as a Christian concept.

A third hypothesis is that a particular soul may inhabit a succession of physical bodies—animal or human—before it is finally released from the "wheel of existence." Upon the death of one body, the soul is "reincarnated" or reborn into another body. This is the teaching of the great oriental religions, Hinduism and Buddhism. It should be noted that both of them look upon reincarnation as a fate to be avoided if possible. The best thing that can happen to a soul, they believe, is to cease to exist as a separate entity, to be absorbed into the "Oversoul" of Infinite Being "like a drop of water disappearing into the sea."

THE CHRISTIAN VIEWPOINT

Finally, there is the Christian viewpoint. It is summarized in the Apostles' Creed by the words: "I believe . . . in the Resurrection of the body: and the Life everlasting." In theory, it is the most widely professed of the four attitudes; in fact, it is the most widely misunderstood.

The first point that should be underscored is that Christianity does NOT go along with the Greek philosophers in drawing a sharp distinction between soul and body. It looks upon the human personality as an integrated whole. This is what the Creed means by resurrection *of the body*. Christians have never thought that physical bodies such as we have now will be restored after death. St. Paul scouted that idea nineteen hundred years ago with the scornful remark that "flesh and blood cannot inherit the Kingdom of God." The "body" to which the Bible and the Creed refer is a spiritual rather than a physical one, and the point is that we shall maintain our separate identities—including our self-awareness and the ability to communicate in some fashion with other beings. In other words, Christianity asserts that what is essential in our humanity—the core of our beings as unique individual persons—will not perish at death, but will enter into a new dimension of life beyond the categories of time and space.

Christianity also differs profoundly from Greek philosophy in that it does NOT regard immortality as an inherent attribute of the human spirit. On the contrary, it teaches that death *is* final for any creature, unless God intervenes to raise him from the dead. This is what "resurrection" means—a positive Divine act of conferring new life where the normal processes of nature have decreed termination and dissolution.

Whether you find the Christian view the most plausible of the four alternatives is, in a sense, beside the point. The Church does not commend this doctrine to you on grounds of self-evident logic. Christian belief in life after death is based entirely on an event—the witnessed fact of Christ's Resurrection—and on his promise that "where I am, you shall be also."

THE PROMISE OF ETERNAL LIFE

The promise of eternal life is held forth unmistakably in the New Testament to all who follow Christ. And Jesus made it clear on several occasions that the test of discipleship is not what a man professes to believe, but how he acts. "Not all those who cry unto me 'Lord, Lord,' shall enter the Kingdom of Heaven," he said, "but those who do the will of God."

The Most Rev. Arthur Michael Ramsey, Archbishop of

Canterbury, drew the logical corollary when he said in a 1961 newspaper interview:

"Heaven is not a place for professing Christians only. Those who have led a good life on earth but found themselves unable to believe in God will not be debarred from Heaven. I expect to meet some present-day atheists there."

But what will happen to those who make no real attempt in this life to do the will of God . . . who turn their backs on Christ because they prefer the easy downhill path of self-indulgence to the rocky way of the Cross?

Will they be summoned before the bar of Divine judgment when they die, and condemned to eternal punishment in hell?

There are passages in the Bible that seem to say so, and this view has been incorporated in the traditional teaching of many Christian bodies, including the Roman Catholic Church and most fundamentalist Protestant denominations.

But there are many other Protestants, including a number of leading theologians, who believe that even the most willful and wicked sinners will get a second chance for repentance after death, and that all persons will eventually be saved. They say that the ultimate redemption of all human souls is the only purpose that can be ascribed to God without detracting either from His sovereignty or from His infinite love for mankind.

"It is God's will, as the New Testament puts it, that all men shall be saved," says the Rev. Dr. W. Norman Pittenger, a prominent Episcopal theologian. "And God's will is in the long run bound to accomplish that for which it sets out. There will be no 'pockets of resistance' left when God has accomplished his final victory over sin, evil and death."

Dr. Pittenger and others note that St. Paul seemed to share this view. In one of his letters to his protégé Timothy, the great Apostle said that God "will have all men to be saved." And he told the Corinthian Christians that "as in Adam all die, even so in Christ shall all be made alive."

Christians who regard universal salvation as a dangerous heresy point to other passages of the New Testament, in which Christ speaks vividly of a final judgment at which the wicked "shall go away into everlasting punishment, but the righteous into life eternal."

They agree that God desires the salvation of all—so much that He has paid the price of reconciliation Himself. But he does not force His grace upon the human creatures whom He has dignified with the gift of free will. He lets them choose light or darkness, and their freedom of choice includes the possibility that they will condemn themselves to eternal separation from Him by finally rejecting His love.

FINAL JUDGMENT OR SECOND CHANCE?

Those who uphold the traditional doctrine of final judgment also contend that belief in universal salvation must lead to disastrous moral consequences, because people will conclude that it doesn't really matter how they live.

The other camp replies that the urgency of moral decisions which men make in this life is not reduced by the possibility that they may get a second chance after death. Believers in universal salvation do not rule out the prospect of judgment and punishment. They simply believe that the nature of God precludes His subjecting even the most wayward sinner to any punishment that is not aimed ultimately at his salvation. *Ultimately* is the key word, and it leaves ample room for prudential fear on the part of those who require such a motivation.

How is the ordinary Protestant layman to choose between the doctrines of eternal punishment and universal salvation?

The United Church of Canada appointed a special commission of forty-three prominent theologians to wrestle with that question. Their report says:

"Perhaps the answer is that we are not meant to choose between them.

"These doctrines are not meant to be understood as theoretical statements which are mutually incompatible," the theologians said. "Rather they are personal statements about our destiny.

"We should not think of the doctrine of universal salvation as a statement about the future which must be true or false, but as an affirmation of the present fact that God seeks to save us and all men.

"We should not think of the doctrine of eternal punishment as a statement about another world which we may accept or reject, but as a warning to us to repent.

"We can never sit back comfortably and decide between universalism and eternal punishment, for these doctrines are speaking about us and to us, calling us to repent, reminding us that no matter how secure we may feel in the faith we still stand under the judgment of God, and reminding us too that no matter how hardened or depraved anyone may be, no sinner who repents is beyond the mercy of God."

10

WILL GOD FORGIVE YOU?

"What must I do to be saved?"

In a letter to the Christians at Rome, the Apostle Paul declared that sinful men are "justified" before God, not by any good works they perform, but solely by putting their faith in Jesus Christ.

His point was that no one can work his passage to heaven by his own efforts. We are all, at heart, too self-centered, too preoccupied with the cares and pleasures of this world, to come within a country mile of deserving to be called children of God. And the more we rely on our own righteousness to make us acceptable to God, the more we find it necessary to rationalize, to water down His demands, to puff up our own good deeds, and to lie to ourselves about our shortcomings.

St. Paul was advising the Romans—and us—to give up the futile attempt at self-justification. Christian living is not a matter of earning enough spiritual merit badges to offset our sins. It is simply a matter of responding—in love, humility, and thankfulness—to the forgiveness which God has bestowed upon us as a free gift which we can never deserve.

WHAT IS JUSTIFICATION BY FAITH?

This is the famous doctrine of "Justification by Faith" which Martin Luther discovered in the writings of St. Paul, and made a cardinal principle of the Protestant Reformation.

As a corrective to the self-righteous pride which afflicts Pharisees of every generation, including our own, it is a very valuable doctrine. We all need to be reminded often that God loves us, not because we are lovable, but because He is merciful.

But Justification by Faith can be a dangerous doctrine, too, if it misleads anyone into thinking that God doesn't really care how we act. The truth is that faith and good works are two sides of the same coin. We cannot truly accept Christ as our Saviour unless we also accept him as our Lord. He put the issue quite clearly:

"If you love me, you will keep my commandments."

And what are his commandments?

In an earlier generation, when many people tended to think of righteous living in terms of rigorous legalism, teachers of Christian ethics usually emphasized that Jesus was much more concerned with positive acts than with "thou shalt nots."

This is quite true. But in our own era of laissez-faire morality, it may be appropriate to point out that Jesus did NOT repeal the Ten Commandments. He explicitly confirmed the ancient moral laws of Judaism against adultery, murder, theft, falsehood, and covetousness. And he interpreted them more strictly than ever before. You don't have to go to bed with a woman to commit adultery with her, he said. You break the commandment as soon as you allow yourself to entertain lustful desires. And it is not enough to refrain from killing your fellow man. You are forbidden even to hate him, and to wish him harm. In case you wish to reread the Ten Commandments, you will find them at the end of this chapter on page 92.

THE COMMAND TO LOVE

Although Christ left plenty of "thou shalt nots" in the moral law, he made it clear that no one could be his disciple merely by avoiding the commission of wrong acts.

"A new commandment I give unto you," he said, "that you love one another."

Here is the whole Christian ethic in a nutshell: all of our relations with other human beings are to be governed by love.

You may think that's easy, or you may think it's impossible, depending on how good-natured you are and how benign you happen to be feeling at this moment. In either case, you're wrong.

The love which Christ commands is *not* easy, even for those fortunate people who are blessed with great natural warmth of heart. And it is not impossible, even for those of us who tend to be crabby and short-tempered. For Christian love is not a vague feeling of affection for someone. It is rather a condition of the heart and will which causes us to seek the welfare of others—including people we don't particularly like, and even people who have done us wrong.

None of us can do this with any degree of success under

91

his own steam. It is possible to all of us, however, if we open our hearts to Christ in faith and allow *his* love to flow through us. This may sound like a high-flown figure of speech, but it is actually as close as words can come to describing a very practical reality which countless Christians experience every day. If you learn to rely entirely on the indwelling Spirit of Christ to supply the loving-kindness and concern for others which you know yourself to lack, you will be amazed at how many good things God can accomplish for others through you.

THE TWO ASPECTS OF CHRISTIAN LOVE

There are two hallmarks of Christian love which stand out vividly in the New Testament.

First, it is concerned with the *whole person*.

A shockingly large number of church members seem to have the idea that they are required to take an interest in their neighbor's spiritual welfare, but are under no special obligation to care about his health, happiness, wages, or working conditions. This is directly contrary to Christ's teaching.

In the twenty-fifth chapter of St. Matthew's Gospel, he tells us, in vivid metaphors, that the way to show love for him is to feed the hungry, clothe the naked, shelter the homeless, befriend the friendless. He comes close to saying that such acts of mercy—directed at the mundane, earthly needs of our fellow man—are the only thing that will really count for much at the final judgment. Since you really ought to read this whole passage, you'll find it reproduced at the end of this chapter.

The second hallmark of Christian love is that it embraces *all persons*.

In the parable of the Good Samaritan, another parable so important you may wish to turn to page 103 for its full text, Jesus made clear that we are commanded to care not only for our relatives, friends, neighbors, and countrymen, but also for strangers and foreigners whom we've never met and with whom we have none of the ordinary bonds of human sympathy.

CHRISTIANS AND FOREIGN AID

This lesson has evidently not penetrated very deeply into the thinking of many American church members. Each year, the major religious organizations go before Congress to plead for a greater allotment of America's national abundance to the task of raising living standards for the two thirds of the human race who are chronically hungry. And just as regularly, congressmen are deluged with letters from self-designated church members who say that they don't want any more of their tax money "wasted" on foreign aid.

Whether the foreign-aid program is being wisely administered, or whether any particular aspect of it is worthwhile, are questions on which men of good will may differ. But it is hard to see how anyone calling himself a Christian can proclaim his indifference to human suffering just because the sufferers happen to live in a distant land.

Some church members seek to justify their hostility to foreign aid by saying that they prefer to express their concern through private channels rather than a government program. That is fine—if true. But the statistical reports of the National Council of Churches show that the average American church member gives *less than $2.00 a year* to help provide doctors, nurses, schools, and other forms of ministry for people who are served by Christian missions abroad. With our national income nudging $500 billion a year, private agencies such as Church World Service have a difficult time raising as much as $5 million to finance their overseas relief work.

Foreign aid is only one of many contemporary problems which test our understanding of and obedience to Christ's command that we "carry one another's burdens." The Negro's struggle for equal opportunity and human dignity is a continuing challenge to every white-skinned Christian to put up or shut up about loving thy neighbor. So is the perennial effort to improve the plight of migrant farm workers. In any session of Congress, dozens of other issues arise in which the American people, through their elected representatives, must choose whether to pause and bind up the wounds of a suffering segment of humanity, or pass by on the other side. Each time the choice is made, those who call themselves Christians should remember the New Testament's sharp question:

"If anyone has the world's goods and sees his brother in need, yet closes his heart against him, how does God's love abide in him?"

The "liberal heresy"

Although we badly need to apply Christ's law of love in our corporate response to social problems, we must beware of falling into what someone has aptly called "the liberal heresy." The liberal heresy consists of becoming so preoccupied with the service of "mankind" that we neglect to behave with ordinary kindness and decency toward the individual specimens of humanity who are fated to live and work in our immediate vicinity. Most of us are guilty of it at times, and we often compound the sin by feeling that we have a "right" to be a bit nasty or selfish in our private relationships since we're doing so much public good. Thus we are both unloving and prideful—the two things that Jesus detested most.

The adage "charity begins at home" does not come from the Bible, as many mistakenly believe. But it contains a valid Christian insight—if we remember that the word "charity" as used in this old saying (and throughout the King James Version of the Bible) really means Christian love. Unless I act lovingly toward the particular man who is literally my brother, there is not much point to Christ's teaching that all men are brothers.

Know your own ways of being mean

Few of the people who read this book are likely to be overtly cruel to their wives, husbands, children, friends, and secretaries. But there are many subtle ways of inflicting hurt upon another human being. A husband who would not humiliate his wife by having an affair with another woman may yet break her heart simply by withdrawing from her emotionally and leaving her to face middle age empty and alone. Parents who lavish everything (including time and attention) on their children may still drive them to self-despair by expecting them to "succeed" beyond their capabilities. A woman who is usually quite gentle may draw blood from a friend to feed her own ego. I know of a famous clergyman who is regarded as a saint by everyone except his secretary, whom he torments daily with picayune complaints.

Perhaps your particular form of meanness is not reflected in any of the above examples. But no matter: *you* know what it is. And you have probably wondered, like the rest of us, why you do it and how you can learn to be loving in your everyday personal relationships.

Jesus said that the secret lies in *forgiving*.

The reason we hurt other human beings, in most cases, is that we are consciously or unconsciously trying to "get even" for a hurt that has been inflicted on us. The person we choose for a victim is not necessarily the one responsible for our own suffering. Once we've built up a head of hostility, we're apt to take it out on anyone who is vulnerable—such as a mate, child or subordinate.

COULD YOU PRAY FOR A FIRST-CLASS STINKER?

It does no good to tell yourself that you "ought not" do it. Nor does it help to be bitterly remorseful after you've done it. The only way to avoid the deadly build-up of hate inside of you is to forgive the people who do you wrong, immediately, completely and wholeheartedly.

Jesus talked about forgiveness a great deal. The importance he attached to it as the key to human relations is reflected in the radical doctrine which he laid down in the Sermon on the Mount:

"You have learned that our forefathers were told, 'an eye for an eye and a tooth for a tooth.' But what I tell you is this: Do not set yourself against the man who wrongs you. If someone slaps you on your right cheek, turn and offer him your left. If a man wants to sue you for your shirt, let him have your coat as well. If a man in authority makes you go one mile, go with him two . . . Love your enemies, pray for your persecutors, bless those who curse you, do good to those who hate you."

Strong words. But the most eloquent lesson in forgiveness which Jesus gave to his disciples was his own example.

As he hung in agony upon the Cross, the wooden nails tearing at the flesh of his hands and feet, he looked down upon the sneering men who had crucified him, and prayed:

"Father, forgive them. They know not what they do."

But, you are thinking, I'm just *not* that good. Of course, you're not. None of us are. But Christ is. And his forgiving Spirit can flood our mean little hearts and transform them in the most remarkable way, if we will only allow it to happen.

When someone does you wrong, intentionally or otherwise, don't waste time feeling sorry for yourself, or thinking how unfair, ungrateful, or unreasonable it was, or how much the offender deserves a comeuppance. Just offer the hurt to God, as if it were a sacrifice you were bringing to his altar (which, in the most profound sense, it is) and ask him to help you accept it and forgive the person who did it to you, in the spirit of Christ. To make sure you are really forgiving, and not going through pious motions, try to find some little act of kindness which you can do for the person who hurt you—*without his knowing that you did it.* (Otherwise, you may be nice just to make him feel like a heel, which is not the idea.) One thing you can always do for people in secret is to pray for them. It is quite incredible the changes that take place in your heart—and possibly in his, as well—when you pray sincerely for God's blessing on a first-class stinker who deserves, by all human standards, to be kicked in the teeth.

YOU CAN'T HAVE IT BOTH WAYS

But what if I don't really want to forgive? What if I insist on standing up for my rights, and demanding fair play?

That's your privilege. And God will give you just what

you ask. This is the most terrifying promise that Jesus made. Anyone who insists on putting justice above mercy will get his way. But of course, he can't have it both ways. If he wants to judge others by a strict standard of right and wrong, then he must expect to be judged by the same standard. Jesus tried to get this point across to his disciples by including, in the model prayer he taught them, the petition: "Forgive us our trespasses, *as we forgive those who trespass against us.*" But the disciples found it as difficult as we do to believe that Jesus really meant all he said about the paramount importance of a forgiving spirit. Once Peter asked:

"Lord, how often shall my brother sin against me, and I forgive him? As many as seven times?"

"I do not say to you seven times," Jesus replied, "but seventy times seven."

Then he told the disciples a story—one of those magnificent little anecdotes of his which we now call by the portentous name of "parables"—about a king who wished to settle accounts with his servants.

Here is the story, as it is recorded in the New English Bible translation of the eighteenth chapter of Matthew:

At the outset of the reckoning, there appeared before the king "a man whose debt ran into millions."

"Since he had no means of paying, his master ordered him to be sold to meet the debt, with his wife, his children and everything he had.

"The man fell prostrate at his master's feet. 'Be patient with me,' he said, 'and I will pay in full.' And the master was so moved with pity that he let the man go and remitted the debt.

"But no sooner had the man gone out than he met a

fellow-servant who owed him a few pounds. And catching hold of him he gripped him by the throat and said, 'Pay me what you owe.'

"The man fell at his fellow-servant's feet, and begged him, 'be patient with me, and I will pay you.' But he refused, and had him jailed until he should pay the debt. The other servants were deeply distressed when they saw what had happened, and they went to their master and told him the whole story. He accordingly sent for the man.

"'You scoundrel,' he said to him. 'I remitted the whole of your debt when you appealed to me; were you not bound to show your fellow-servant the same pity as I showed to you?' And so angry was the master that he condemned the man to torture until he should pay the debt in full."

Jesus concluded the story with a blunt warning:

"And that is how my heavenly Father will deal with you, unless you each forgive your brother from your hearts."

FORGIVE YOUR BROTHER FOR WHAT HE IS

Jesus taught that we are to forgive our brother, not only for what he *does*, but for what he *is*. He may be an atheist or an adulterer or a drunk or a braggart or something else that we consider to be reprehensible. But it is not up to us to judge him. Only God knows how to apportion the blame for his estate between his free will and the circumstances which have borne upon him. Once in a great while, Christian love may require us to admonish a brother, and to try to help him see where he is heading. But of all the tasks of Christian compassion, none should be undertaken more sparingly or with greater fear and trembling. Whenever we undertake it, we should hear in the back of our minds the question Jesus asked:

"Why do you look at the speck of sawdust in your brother's eye, with never a thought for the great plank in your own? . . . You hypocrite! First take the plank out of your own eye, and then you will see clearly to take the speck out of your brother's."

THREE TEXTS YOU MAY WANT TO REREAD

1. The Ten Commandments

The Ten Commandments are recorded in the twentieth chapter of the Book of Exodus.

Here they are, in the Revised Standard Version translation:

"And God spoke all these words, saying,

" 'I am the Lord your God, who brought you out of the land of Egypt, out of the house of bondage.

" 'You shall have no other gods before me.

" 'You shall not make yourself a graven image, or any likeness of anything that is in heaven above, or that is in the earth beneath, or that is in the water under the earth; you shall not bow down to them or serve them . . .

" 'You shall not take the name of the Lord your God in vain . . .

" 'Remember the sabbath day, to keep it holy . . .

" 'Honor your father and your mother . . .

" 'You shall not kill.

" 'You shall not commit adultery.

" 'You shall not steal.

" 'You shall not bear false witness against your neighbor.

" 'You shall not covet your neighbor's house; you shall

not covet your neighbor's wife, or his manservant, or his maidservant, or his ox, or his ass, or anything that is your neighbor's."

Although Protestants, Catholics and Jews are agreed that there are ten commandments (they have to agree on this because the Bible says specifically there are ten), it is an interesting fact that they have never been able to get together on the numbering. Jews regard the opening sentence, "I am the Lord your God, etc.," as a separate commandment. Protestants usually lump it with the following sentence, "You shall have no other gods before me." Catholics split the final admonitions against covetousness into two commandments, and include the stricture against graven images with the general prohibition against "other gods."

There is no way of settling the argument, since the original Hebrew text is not broken up into paragraphs like our modern Bibles. Nor is there any real need to number the commandments. "You shall not commit adultery" is a forthright moral law whether it is regarded as the Sixth Commandment or the Seventh.

2. The Last Judgment

The twenty-fifth chapter of St. Matthew's Gospel contains a vivid word picture of the Last Judgment which Jesus painted for his disciples. In reading it, bear in mind that parables, as used by the Jewish teachers of Jesus' day, were told to drive home *one basic moral point*. The imagery of the setting is not meant to be taken literally, nor should the parable be cited as a "proof text" in support of one theological view of final judgment. (See Chapter 9.)

Here is the New English Bible translation:

"When the Son of Man comes in his glory, and all the angels with him, he will sit in state on his throne, with all the nations gathered before him.

"He will separate men into two groups, as a shepherd separates the sheep from the goats, and he will place the sheep on his right hand and the goats on his left.

"Then the king will say to those on his right hand, 'You have my Father's blessing; come, enter and possess the kingdom that has been ready for you since the world was made. For when I was hungry, you gave me food; when thirsty, you gave me drink; when I was a stranger you took me into your home, when naked you clothed me; when I was ill you came to my help, when in prison you visited me.'

"Then the righteous will reply, 'Lord, when was it that we saw you hungry and fed you, or thirsty and gave you drink, a stranger and took you home, or naked and clothed you? When did we see you ill or in prison and come to visit you?'

"And the king will answer, 'I tell you this: anything you did for one of my brothers here, however humble, you did for me.'

"Then he will say to those on his left hand, 'the curse is upon you; go from my sight to the eternal fire that is ready for the devil and his angels. For when I was hungry you gave me nothing to eat, when thirsty nothing to drink; when I was a stranger you gave me no home, when naked you did not clothe me; when I was ill and in prison you did not come to my help.'

"And they too will reply, 'Lord, when was it that we saw you hungry or thirsty or a stranger or naked or ill or in prison, and did nothing for you?'

"And he will answer, 'I tell you this: anything you did

not do for one of these, however humble, you did not do for me.'

3. *The Good Samaritan*

Jesus told the parable of the Good Samaritan in reply to questions put to him by a lawyer, who cited the commandment to "love thy neighbor as thyself."

"And who is my neighbor?" asked the lawyer, anxious, as members of his profession always are, to get down to specifics.

Jesus' reply is found in the tenth chapter of St. Luke's Gospel. Here is the Revised Standard Version translation:

"A man was going down from Jerusalem to Jericho, and he fell among robbers, who stripped him and beat him, and departed, leaving him half dead.

"Now by chance a priest was going down that road; and when he saw him he passed by on the other side.

"So likewise a Levite, when he came to the place and saw him, passed by on the other side.

"But a Samaritan, as he journeyed, came to where he was; and when he saw him, he had compassion, and went to him and bound up his wounds, pouring on oil and wine; then he set him on his own beast and brought him to an inn, and took care of him.

"And the next day he took out two denarii and gave them to the innkeeper, saying, 'Take care of him; and whatever more you spend, I will repay you when I come back.'"

After telling this vivid little story, Jesus looked at the lawyer and asked which of the three men had "proved neighbor to the man who fell among the robbers."

"The one who showed mercy on him," replied the lawyer.

"Go and do likewise," said Jesus.

11

WORK AT BEING A CHRISTIAN

How long does it take to become a Christian?
A moment—and a lifetime.

Some Protestant bodies place a good deal of emphasis on
the moment of "conversion" at which a person consciously
accepts Christ as his Lord and Saviour. And it is certain
that many great Christians—among them, St. Paul, St.
Augustine, and John Wesley—have been able to pinpoint
a precise moment at which their lives were changed.

But it is equally certain that many Christians never un-
dergo a dramatic conversion experience. Some of them
"grow up in the faith" and can never remember any time
in their lives when they did not think of Jesus as Lord.
Others spend anxious years of seeking, and move from
doubt to faith by such imperceptible stages that they cannot look back and say of any particular moment, "This is
when it happened."

However we may set out on the path of pilgrimage, we
spend a lifetime walking it. There are no rest stops, no

plateaus at which we can flop down and say that we've gone far enough. At the beginning, God accepts us in all of our sinfulness and selfishness. But this does not mean that He is content to have us remain in that state. We are all, in the New Testament's terrifying phrase, "called to be saints." Our Father knows our weaknesses even better than we do, and He does not expect us to become saints overnight. But He does demand that we keep moving in that direction, or as the good old Methodist phrase puts it, that we continue "groaning towards perfection." At each step of the journey, the question that really matters is not whether we are a little farther along than some of our friends and neighbors, but how far we have progressed since yesterday.

THERE IS NO EASY WAY

This is a dreadfully tiresome prospect. It would be much easier to get "saved" all at once and be done with it, so that we could turn our attention to other things. But Jesus did not say, "Come to me and get it over with." He said:

"If any man would come after me, let him take up his cross *daily* and follow me."

Daily is the key word. Our commitment to Christ, however genuine and wholehearted it may be today, must be renewed tomorrow . . . and the day after that . . . and the day after that . . . until the path comes at last to the river.

Moreover, there are a lot of rocks strewn along the path on which we are bound to stumble. One of them is doubt.

In the very first chapter of this book, you found an unequivocal statement that it is possible to be *sure* of God. I'm not welshing on that in the last chapter. Any pilgrim who honestly seeks God will find him, and will experience periods—perhaps moments at first, later hours or even days in which he apprehends the reality of God so directly and overwhelmingly that he can truly speak, not of believing, but of *knowing*.

But the bright hours of clear vision are always followed, sooner or later, by dark and groping periods, when God seems far away or totally unreal, and the whole Christian story begins to sound improbable. I am much too green a pilgrim myself to understand *why* this happens. Sometimes it seems to stem from physical and emotional fatigue—a pointed reminder that Christian self-discipline entails a proper concern for the body as well as the soul.

GETTING THROUGH THE "DRY PERIODS"

One thing I do know from reading the lives of the great saints of the past, and from talking to some who are alive today: these "dry periods" are the common lot of *all* Christian pilgrims, and no one ever reaches a point where he is beyond the temptation to doubt and despair.

Even Jesus, as he hung on the cross, cried out: "My God, My God, why hast Thou forsaken me?" In that awesome moment, Our Lord drank the dregs of humanity's cup, and identified himself most fully with our condition.

George Macdonald, the saintly nineteenth-century Scottish preacher whose writings have been rescued from obscurity by C. S. Lewis, has a theory about the role which dry periods play in spiritual development. God, he says, "wants to make us in his own image, *choosing* the good, *refusing* the evil."

"How should he effect this if he were *always* moving us from within, as he does at divine intervals, towards the beauty of his holiness?" Macdonald asks. Thus, he says, God sometimes seems to withdraw from us, to leave us temporarily without the comfort and strengthening of His Spirit.

Macdonald also has good advice for getting through dry periods:

"Troubled soul, thou art not bound to feel but thou art bound to arise. God loves thee whether thou feelest or not. Thou canst not love when thou wilt, but thou art bound to fight the hatred in thee to the last.

"Try not to feel good when thou art not good, but cry to him who is good. He changes not because thou changest. Nay, he has an especial tenderness of love towards thee for that thou art in the dark and hast no light, and his heart is glad when thou dost arise and say, 'I will go to my Father.'

"Fold the arms of thy faith, and wait in quietness until light goes up in thy darkness. Fold the arms of thy faith, I say, but not of thy action. Bethink thee of something that thou oughtest to do, and go to do it, if it be but the sweeping of a room, or the preparing of a meal, or a visit to a friend.

"Heed not thy feelings: do thy work."

Because we establish a false equation between feelings and faith, we are apt to find ourselves, during dry periods, asking anxiously whether we "really" believe in God or have just been living in a comforting illusion.

Macdonald has an antidote for this too:

"Instead of asking yourself whether you believe or not, ask yourself whether you have this day done one thing because he said, *do it*, or once abstained because he said, *do not do it* . . .

"Faith is . . . the leaving of your way, your objects, your self, and the taking of his and him; the leaving of your trust in men, in money, in opinion, in character, in atonement itself, and *doing as he tells you.*

"I can find no words strong enough for the weight of this obedience."

We said in the last chapter that true faith leads to obedience. What George Macdonald is saying is that the reverse is also true. Obedience leads to faith. Live faithfully by the little bit of light you now have, and you will be given more.

This is a cardinal fact about spiritual growth on which all of the great souls of the ages seem to agree.

"To all those who are perplexed in any way whatsoever, who wish for light but cannot find it, one precept must be given—*obey*," said Cardinal Newman.

OVERCOMING YOUR DOUBTS

The English theologian, F. W. Robertson, wrote:

"There are hours, and they come to all of us at some period of life or other, when the hand of Mystery seems to lie heavy on the soul—when some life-shock scatters existence, leaves it a blank and dreary waste henceforth forever . . . In such moments you doubt all—whether Christianity be true: whether Christ was Man, or God, or a beautiful fable . . . In such an hour what remains? I reply, *obedience.* Leave those thoughts for the present. Act—be merciful and gentle—honest . . . try to do good to others: be true to the duty that you know . . . And by all the laws of the human heart, by the word of God, you shall not be left to doubt."

Obey . . . take up your cross . . . deny yourself . . . it all sounds very hard.

It *is* hard. Anyone who tells you differently is peddling spiritual soothing syrup, not real Christianity.

And yet, in a strangely paradoxical way, it is also easy.

With every cross that we lift in obedience to Christ comes the strength to carry it. It is always a package deal. If you should ever find yourself genuinely unable to bear a particular cross, you can be sure that it was one you devised for yourself rather than one which Christ called you to carry. That is one reason why it is a great mistake to anticipate your crosses, and to ponder anxiously whether you would really be able to make this or that particular sacrifice for him. If he wants you to do something, he'll make it possible for you to do it, but the grace he provides comes only with the task, and cannot be stockpiled beforehand. We are dependent on him from hour to hour, and the greater our awareness of this fact, the less likely we are to faint or fail in a crisis. "When I am weak," said St. Paul, "then I am strong."

THANKING GOD FOR YOUR TROUBLES

The nearness of Christ when there are real and heavy crosses to be borne can be felt so strongly that people who are very far indeed from sainthood have found themselves spontaneously and sincerely thanking God for troubles, because those troubles have brought with them the infinitely precious awareness that "underneath are the everlasting arms."

"Take my yoke upon you," Jesus said. But in the next breath he added:

"My yoke is easy and my burden is light."

He also said:

"Come to me, all who labor and are heavy-laden, and I will give you rest."

And he promised:

"Lo, I am with you always, even unto the end."

With such a Companion, it is a joy to walk the rocky path of pilgrimage.